Understand
The Ecology of the Bible
An Introductory Atlas

PAUL H. WRIGHT

cartaJerusalem

First published in 2018 by
CARTA Jerusalem

Photographs: Paul H. Wright
 (unless otherwise indicated)

Cartography: Carta Jerusalem

ISBN: 978-965-220-897-2

Printed in Israel

CONTENTS

MAPS

(overleaf) The plains of Jericho as depicted on the Madaba Map, 6th century A.D. The mosaic artist depicted the oasis of Jericho as the city of palm trees (Deut 34:3; Judg 3:13). It was across this plain that Joshua led Israel into Canaan, his people's promised land. Ironically, the writer of Genesis 13:10 had likened the same region to the land of Egypt.

A. "IN HIS HAND IS THE LIFE OF EVERY LIVING THING" — JOB 12:10

Springtime growth in the hill country of Ephraim.

The Bible is a book of life. By its own idiom it is "living and active" (Heb 4:12), a divine word that brings life and empowers life. The Bible teems with life: creative life, striving life, flourishing life and redemptive life. It is preoccupied with life: a living God creates living beings which themselves are fruitful and multiply; an ongoing cycle of seasons renews life; even death is a natural transition from this-life to after-life (Gen 1:11–12, 22, 28; 8:22; Ezek 37:1–10). The Bible describes life the way it is, but also the way it should be—and this not just for the human species but the entire created order (eg. Isa 35:1–2; 55:12–13; Rev 21:1). This predisposition for life should not be surprising, for the unpronounceable personal name of God himself, represented by the Tetragramaton *YHWH* and rendered into English as LORD, derives from the Hebrew verb "to live." As such, it is an indicator of an Identity that expresses the absolute fullness of life, immediate, present, transcendent and essential. Of course the significance of this is grasped only when we remember that the names of the pagan deities that filled the world out of which the Bible arose were names of elements of nature (e.g., Anu, "sky;" Re, "sun;" Yam, "sea" or Hadad, "thunderer"), or names that reflected specific human behavior or institutions (e.g., Baal, "master;" Molech, perhaps "the reigning one;" Kothar weHasis, "adroit and cunning;" or Mot, "death"). Not so for YHWH, the One Who Is (Ex 3:14) and From Whom Life Flows:

> Ask the beasts, and they will teach you;
> the birds of the air, and they will tell you;
> or the plants of the earth, and they will teach you;
> and the fish of the sea will declare to you.
> Who among all these does not know

> *that the hand of the LORD has done this?*
> *In his hand is the life of every living thing*
> *and the breath of all mankind.*
>
> Job 12:7–10

It is only natural, then, that the Bible is a book about life: its origins, its present reality and its future hope. The world of created life—of nature—fills the biblical text. And nature is not only the locus of the biblical narrative, it provides an endless set of images through which greater realities are to be understood.

One of the things that makes the Bible itself alive is that it is fully immersed in the world of nature, a world that is real, that can be marked on a map, that can be visited and can be lived in. The reality of nature, and the metaphors that it inspires, infuse every aspect of the sacred text, from Genesis in the Hebrew Bible to Revelation in the New Testament. For this reason, a first-hand awareness of the landed context of the Bible provides a base line from which we, as informed readers, can build our understandings of the history and world view of ancient Israel, and from that, theologies that continue to speak today.

The Bible holds two axioms in a kind of balanced tension: God is transcendent, but he is also intimately involved in creation. This kind of both/and thinking, presupposed by the writers[1] of the Bible, has been held by many of its readers in the millennia since. Together, these necessarily paired concepts provide a helpful framework in which to set the topic *Ecology of the Bible*. The subject matter is much larger than a mere catalog description of the plant and animal life mentioned on the pages of Scripture, or even that of the living environment of the lands of the eastern Mediterranean,

Abraham was called to journey to a land that he did not know. In its bare immensities he begat a people who expressed their understanding of God through categories that arose from, yet transcended, their home.

as helpful as these may be. Rather, the human story, as complex and interventionist as it is, must also play a role. How was the created, or natural, order regarded by the people who inhabited the world of the Bible? What role did nature play in human existence in ancient Israel, not only for the mundane tasks of providing daily subsistence but also in fostering environments in which people could form social, political and economic structures that made for responsible living? How does the world of nature come to provide such an inexhaustible set of images that describe spiritual realities? And what practical implications might be had for us as Bible readers today, whether we live in the same lands as the people of the Bible, or elsewhere?

As part of this task we have the opportunity to gather and synthesize data that can help us understand how people from the world of the Bible thought about the God-made natural world in which they lived, their own "theologies of the land" so to speak. Land in its largest sense is not just *terra firma* but sea and sky as well, and as such is the locus of the interrelationship between all of the living things that call the earth's terrestrial, watery and airy terrains home. Yet while each of these are elements of the created order, the story of ancient Israel is primarily that of a people at home on dry land, a place whose border was the sea (Josh 15:5, 12) and whose airy expanse was unreachable (Job 37:18; Isa 44:24). The sea may have been a gateway or thoroughfare for the Philistines, the Phoenicians or the Greeks, but for the Israelites it was something beyond which normal human activity could take place (Ps 107:23–32; Isa 57:20–21; Rev 21:1). It and the realm of the sky were held in awe; land, on the other hand, was familiar, and home. The ecology of the Bible quite naturally, then, focuses on flora and fauna that were encountered on a day to day basis by the people of ancient Israel, and in particular that which grew or lived on the specific portion of dry land in which ancient Israel lived.

The Hebrew word *eretz*, "land," is the fifth most frequently used noun in the Hebrew Bible, after *YHWH* (LORD), *ben* ("son"), *Elohim* ("God") and *melekh* ("king"). This combination of nouns is instructive, suggesting that there was (and is) an essential trinity (to borrow a word that has theological weight) comprised of God, progeny and land that somehow forms the basis of a life that is at the same time earthly and spiritual, belonging yet custodial, given and received. Land certainly can be a theological concept, but for the people of the Bible it was first a geographical one, an arena in which life could be lived in peace, shalom, the way it was meant to be:

So Judah and Israel lived in safety, every man under his vine and fig tree, from Dan to Beersheba, all the days of Solomon.

1 Kings 4:25

Although *eretz* is most often used in the Hebrew Bible in connection with a particular, bounded area that became the homeland of the people of ancient Israel (e.g., Gen 12:1; 15:18; Deut 1:21), its sweep of territory was much larger, encompassing that of "all the nations of the earth (*eretz*)" (Gen 18:18; Jer 25:26; Zech 4:10, 14). Thinking inclusively, this prompts readers of the Bible to consider how principles of the ecology of place, understood first within the context of the land of ancient Israel, can be expanded to include the whole of the created order. We might argue, in fact, that a full-orbed theology of land should take into account concepts of place that apply *wherever* a Bible reader's own locality might be, whether it is a place that is owned, used, or simply visited by oneself or by others. The Bible's own emphasis on the created order as the locus of the divine-human encounter shows us that *place*—whether it is the land of ancient Israel or somewhere else—gives order to human existence, providing a sense of connectedness and belonging.[2] When land is reduced to political concepts of ownership, rights or control, the result is a conversation that ignores or overrides the more essential aspects of what land, as a God-made place for human fulfillment, can be, and the interconnected relationship of all living things (the *eco-* of ecology) on it.[3]

* * * * *

We can identify three reasons why understanding the ecology of the Bible is important for Bible readers today: 1) Flora and fauna are the basic living stuff of creation and as such provide the natural context of the biblical story; 2) the daily life of an ancient Israelite was embedded in the natural world in which he or she lived; and 3) the natural elements of the world of the Bible serve as tangible images of realities that transcend nature, primarily the God-people dynamic about which the Bible was written in the first place. Each of these needs further explanation.

First, and without any particular fanfare, the Bible's own introduction states that God created flora and fauna on days three, five and six of the creation week (Gen 1:9–13, 20–31), then chose to interact in a personal way with the whole host of living elements that he had made. The biblical act of creation assumes a kind of shared intimacy in the created order between people and God. This intimacy is seen in the subsequent narrative line of the Bible, a long and entangled story in which God interacted with people in specific places and in which the world of nature played a paramount role. If there is something that the Bible is *not*, it is that it is *not abstract* or separated from real life but rather wholly immersed in the affairs of human beings. And the dominance of God over people (as the Creator-created relationship demands) echoes the divinely apportioned dominance of people over the rest of creation. "Subdue *it*," the writer of Genesis 1:28 intoned, and the rest of the Bible unpacks that terse statement in a way that shows that submission ought to

reflect responsible care for the world's multitude of living beings, human and otherwise, living together wherever they may be. Eden was "adequate and bounteous" (in the words of Elmer Martens[4]), and as such provides an introductory template for how we should see God's care for land and people throughout the biblical story.

Because the land of ancient Israel was a gift[5] (Ex 6:8; Deut 5:31; 6:10–11, etc.) and a blessing (Deut 11:10–12, etc.) but also a point of temptation[6] (Deut 8:11–20; 32:15–43; Ps 78:54–58), living in that land demanded a specific kind of lifestyle that was reflected by the moral, civil and cultic (or, ritual) provisions of Torah. These lifestyle obligations were (and are) marked annually with a set of festivals that were not only tied to the times of harvest in the land where ancient Israel lived but also linked to Israel's great foundational epic: *Pesach* (Passover) marked the beginning of the barley harvest and the Exodus from Egypt; *Shavuot* (Weeks) the end of the wheat harvest and the giving of Torah on Mount Sinai; and *Succot* (Tabernacles) the harvest of summer fruit and the provision for God's people during their long years of Wilderness Wandering (Ex 23:14–17; Deut 16:1–17). Each, in Jewish memory, is also a Sabbath, a super-sizing of the weekly Sabbath that itself was grounded, according to Exodus 20:8–11, in creation. With these ever-recurring moments in time, celebration of the order of divinely-made, human-enjoyed creation comes full circle every year. In the biblical conception, every living thing would grow in blessing if its human inhabitants kept Torah, but would wither away, cursed, on a land that had become as hard as iron if not (Deut 28:1–24; Isa 33:8–9; 35:1–2). All of this subsumes the ideas of ownership, control and rights to those of conservation, preservation and responsibility.

Second, an understanding of the ecology of the Bible is important for Bible readers because the living environment of the Bible is not

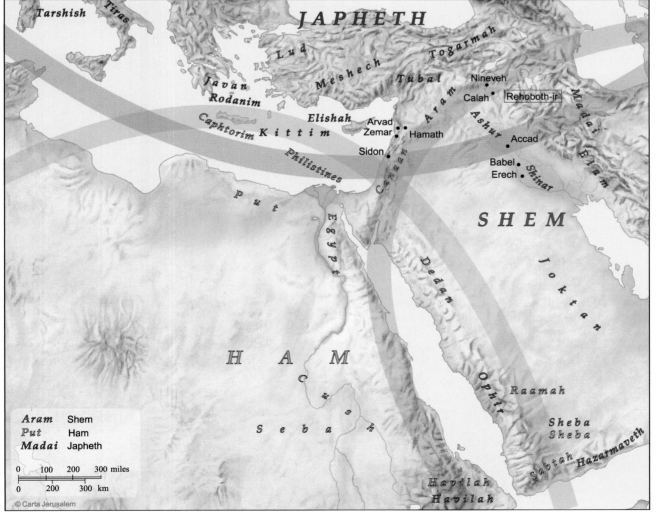

JAPHETH

Tarshish · Tiras · Lud · Javan · Rodanim · Meshech · Togarmah · Tubal · Elishah · Kittim · Caphtorim · Arvad · Zemar · Hamath · Sidon · Philistines · Canaan · Put · Egypt

Nineveh · Calah · Rehoboth-ir · Ashur · Accad · Madai · Elam · Babel · Erech · Shinar

SHEM

Dedan · Joktan · Ophir · Raamah · Sheba · Sheba · Sabtah · Hazarmaveth · Havilah · Havilah · Seba

HAM · Cush

Aram — Shem
Put — Ham
Madai — Japheth

0   100   200   300 miles
0   200   300 km

© Carta Jerusalem

A succah in the house of a member of the Samaritan community on Mt. Gerizim. A Samaritan succah is a table canopy made of the summer fruit of the land.

(below) A sheep slaughter in Wadi Rum, Jordan. The slaughter is done by students of biblical ecology while an attentive Bedouin stands by.

New). Because the world of the Bible was essentially a small village, rural and agricultural world, the rhythm of farming and shepherding lifestyles is everywhere present in the biblical text. Here we can gain much by looking at practices of agriculture (both grain farming and horticulture), of herding and stock-raising, and of the use of plants and animals for domestic purposes in ancient Israel. The language is technical and the details immense (as might be expected for any aspect of the human endeavor), but our harvest proportionate to the effort made.

The intrinsic value of every living thing within the functional environment of the biblical world was placed into a set of hierarchies keyed to what was most beneficial to people (this is the "subdue it" of Genesis 1:28). Hence, within the biblical narrative, flora and fauna are ranked in terms of what is useful for human life (e.g., the seven species of Deuteronomy 8:8, especially as they are related to the harvest festivals, as well as herd animals for food or sacrifice, and plants used for medicines and healing) and what is predator or harmful (e.g., lions, serpents, scorpions, thorns, thistles and the like; Gen 3:18; Ps 7:2; Eccl 10:8; Rev 9:5). The cycle of life and death is assumed: animals die so that people can live (the reality that life is in the blood is not just a Temple axiom), while total harmony between all living things in a way that "the wolf will lie down with the lamb" (Isa 11:6) will happen only in the world to come.

Third, for most Bible readers an understanding of the ecology of the Bible is not significant for its own sake or even because it forms the context of the biblical story but because the plant and animal life of the Bible offers a vibrant set of images (or, icons) that help us picture God, ourselves and others, as well as the lively dynamic that makes for the intersection of divine and human life. Vine; olive tree; sheep; fish; lion; snake; thorns—biblical images leap from the ground onto the page and into our hearts. As one of many thousands of biblical examples:

For as the rain and snow come down from heaven
   and do not return there without watering the earth
 and making it bear and sprout,
    and furnishing seed to the sower and bread to the eater,
    so will My word be which goes forth from My mouth.
It will not return to Me empty

just a backdrop to the larger story of people and God. Rather, plants and animals, like the land on which they grow and feed and live and die, are an integral part of the grand narrative of Scripture. It is axiomatic, though oft-forgotten in a modern world of virtual realities, that the constituent elements of the history of ancient Israel are important *precisely* because the Judeo-Christian faiths are rooted in the actual experiences of people with God in real places, the scenes of which were (and remain) filled with all kinds of living things. A large view emphasizes portions of the Bible that provide a holistic understanding of how life ought best be lived in the land given to ancient Israel. But immersed within the Former and Latter Prophets, many of the Writings (especially Psalms, Proverbs and Job), the book of Deuteronomy and the Gospels are countless details of what everyday life was like for individual Israelites (in the time of the Old Testament) and, later, Jews (in the time of the

without accomplishing what I desire,
and without succeeding in the matter for which I sent it.

Isaiah 55:10–11

The land and all that it sustains has rightly been termed a kind of "fifth gospel"[7] in which the physicality of place bears witness to the written text, on the analogy that we need to "read" the land in order to "see" the text, rather than the other way around.

Nature imagery comes in a variety of types. One of the most personal is peoples' names. The felt connection between a person's name and his or her identity was much stronger in the biblical world than it is in ours. In the ancient world one's name acknowledged one's *existence*, and as such was believed to reflect something of essence about that person, his or her destiny or character (Gen 17:5; 29:32–35; Matt 1:21–23; etc.). Personal names drawn from nature suggest that characteristics of certain plants and animals were valued as traits that might also be found in people: Deborah ("honey bee"; Judg 4:4), Tamar ("palm tree"; 2 Sam 13:1), Ze'ev ("wolf"; Judg 7:25), Eglah ("heifer"; 2 Sam 3:5), Hagav ("locust"; Ezra 2:46) or Nahash ("snake"; 1 Sam 12:12) are a few of many examples. Some of these, of course, might have been acquired nicknames rather than given names, but the point is the same. Place names, too, are personal, often preserving the names of plants or animals associated with a site, or subsistence activities of the people living there. Again there are many examples, including Migdal-eder ("tower of the flock"; Gen 35:21), Beth-haccerem ("place of the vineyard"; Jer 6:1), Kiriath-jearim ("village of the scrub forest"; 1 Sam 7:1), Jezreel ("God sows"; 1 Kgs 21:1) and Gethsemane ("oil press"; Matt 26:36), as well as nearly every place that Moses and the children of Israel encountered during their years in the Sinai (Num 33:5–49).[8]

Perhaps more familiar are the Bible's parables, which are stories that use vignettes of everyday life to illustrate spiritual or practical truths. One thinks, for instance, of the parable of Jotham, youngest son of Gideon, who likened his oldest brother's seized kingship not to the generous and honored olive tree nor to the sweetness of the fig tree or to the festive blessing of the vine but rather to the bramble—nettlesome, wounding and good only for being burned (Judg 9:7–15; cf. Judg 8:16; Ps 58:9). Equally pointed is the parable of Nathan, David's prophet, who served notice that the king's moral right to reign over Israel hung in the balance because, as it were, he had caused a poor shepherd to lose his only ewe lamb and by consequence, his scant means of livelihood and joy (2 Sam 12:1–6). Jesus' many parables, too, were fully immersed in the world of nature, speaking not only of its many constituent parts (e.g., wheat seed and mustard seed, tares and thorns, fish, sheep or pigs; Matt 13:7, 25–32, 47; 24:32; Lk 15:4, 15) but economic systems grounded in the ecology of the land (e.g., "a sower went out to sow"; "a landowner went out in the early morning to hire laborers for his vineyard"; or "I will tear down my barns and build larger ones and there I will store all my grain"; Matt 13:3; 20:1; Lk 12:18).

Many nature images are found in the Bible's wisdom literature as well. Pithy sayings in the book of Proverbs seek to instill skill in living, where even the smallest bit of the created order has value for the crown ("Go to the ant, O sluggard! Observe its ways and be wise"; Prov 6:6). Of a different nature is the Song of Songs. Whether an allegory of the mutual love between God and his people or an intimate description of that between a man and a woman, the book is a treatise on the vibrant world of nature that enveloped ancient Israel and was ever at hand. The Song of Songs' striking depiction of a bride with hair like a flock of goats, eyes like the pools of Heshbon, teeth like newly shorn ewes, temples like a slice of pomegranate, breasts like two fawns and belly like a heap of wheat is both memorable and clear, at least for those who were immersed in the ecology of the Bible (Song of Songs 4:1–5; 7:2–9).

Yerah-azar ("the moon god is [my] help"), king of Ammon in the late eighth century B.C. and contemporary of Jerusalem's King Hezekiah. The form of the king's name, "X-god is [my] help," is common in the ancient Near East. In this case the god is the moon, the gentle, ever-changing light that rules the wonder of the night. The moon-god dominated desert ecosystems throughout the ancient Near East.

In the poetry of the Psalms and prophets so many more images of nature can be found that a Bible reader only has to close his eyes and point to a verse to hit one: the Psalms begin with a righteous man likened to a tree planted by streams of water (Ps 1:3) and the Prophets end with burnt chaff and calves gamboling from their stall (Mal 4:1–3). From the sparrows that flew into the temple (Ps 84:3) to the reaper cradling newly cut sheaves in his arm (Isa 17:5), all are realities that say something about the relationship of God and people, using the earthy terms of the here (or, then) and now in the process.

The writers of the Bible did not reserve images of the world of nature just for the God-ward glance of people or for the living situation of themselves and others. To the extent that God can be depicted at all, it was, in the minds of the writers of the Bible, through the world that was known to his people. When God appears in theophanic splendor it is as the sunrise over the vast southeastern desert (Deut 33:2; Hab 3:3–4; Ps 104:2), as thunder and lightning on Mount Sinai (Ex 19:16) or as the commanding thunderstorm that hurls itself off the Mediterranean Sea and onto a land that bends under its might (Ps 29:3–9). The author of this book has witnessed all three. Or, the writers of the Bible sometimes chose images of nature that were more mundane—God is, for instance, a rock, (Ps 18:2; 31:2), but also the source (and essence) of living water (Jer 2:13; cf. Jn 7:38). Even God's heavenly messengers are depicted with animal features: "Seraphim stood above Him, each having two wings…" (Isa 6:2). And of course in the great Incarnation of the Christian faith God himself becomes wholly immersed in the earthy, ecologically-filled world of people (Phil 2:6–7).

The Bible, then, is a book to be grasped, and that grasping is facilitated by its being imbedded in a world that, for those who penned its words, was known intuitively, precisely because it was readily at hand. Though we are separated from that world in time and, for many of us, also in place, a careful reading and focused study of both land and text can help restore that world to life. The Book of Life deserves no less.

B. "HOW IS THE LAND? IS IT FAT OR LEAN?" — NUMBERS 13:20

Moses' marching orders to Joshua, Caleb and their ten comrades whom he sent to spy out the land of Canaan were clear:

See what the land is like, whether the people who live in it are strong or weak, whether they are few or many. How is the land in which they live? Is it good or bad? And how are the cities in which they live? Are they like open camps or fortified? How is the land? Is it fat or lean? Are there trees in it, or not?

And make an effort to get some of the fruit of the land!

Numbers 13:18–20

By asking if the land were "fat or lean," Moses of course wanted to know how fertile the intended home for his people would be. Because the words he chose to frame his question more typically reference the fitness of living things rather than land *per se*, the point is clear: The condition of the land and the condition of the things that live on the land are intertwined. This would become a biblical injunction (Deut 28:1–24). For the twelve spies, whose point of reference was the "great and terrible wilderness" of the Sinai from which they had just come (Deut 1:19–20), the land they saw on their run up the hill country watershed was good indeed.

They even brought home some worthy souvenirs: a huge cluster of grapes along with some pomegranates and figs (Num 13:21–24; Deut 1:25). It was late summer, the time of the first ripe grapes (Num 13:20), when the otherwise parched hill country becomes blessed with heavy-laden fruit. Joshua and company noticed the blessing.

Nowadays, first-time visitors to the land of ancient Israel often notice a great disparity between their prior notions of the Bible's assertion that this was a land flowing with milk and honey (e.g., Num 13:27), and actual facts on the ground which, in much of the modern biblical landscape, seem to say otherwise. On the one hand, there is no question that the combination of advanced technology plus backbreaking labor has brought tremendous fertility to large portions of the land today, especially in the Galilee and along the coastal plain but also at many places in the southern and eastern deserts. Modern Israel is indeed a model of technological creativity and efficiency, and its successes with water and soil, crops and herds, are copied by much of the world, including other countries in the Middle East. But even without the advantages of advanced technology, it is obvious that this is a land with great potential for life. For millennia, the local inhabitants—be they grain farmers, horticulturalists or shepherds—made full use of the cycles of nature to coax patterns of livelihood from the ground in ways that can still be seen if we take time to visit the more traditional portions of the hilly and desert areas of the region. It is in practices which still rely primarily on centuries-old technology made of wood, stone and iron and worked by human and animal muscle, rather than by machines of gasoline, rubber and steel, that the reality of the ancient endeavor can best be understood.

The optimism of the biblical writers for the land into which Israel entered to possess is nearly unbounded:

*So I have come down to deliver them from the power of the Egyptians and to bring them up from that land to **a good and spacious land**, to a land flowing with milk and honey.*

Exodus 3:8

*For the LORD your God is bringing you into **a good land**, a land of brooks of water, of fountains and springs, flowing forth in valleys and hills; a land of wheat and barley, of vines and fig trees and pomegranates, a land of olive oil and honey; a land where you will eat food without scarcity, in which you will not lack anything....*

Deuteronomy 8:7–9

When we remember that the term "good" (Heb. *tov*) is that same descriptor used to sum up each of the days on which God created plant and animal life ("God saw that it was good"; Gen 1:12, 17, 21, 25, 31), a careful reader of the Bible is led to consider just how wonderful its writers conceived their land to be—but also to wonder to what extent they were optimists, rather than realists, at heart.

And it isn't just the Bible. The testimony of *The Story of Sinuhe*, a tale from 18th century B.C. Middle Kingdom Egypt, describes the interior of the land of Canaan this way:

THE TRAVELS OF THE SPIES

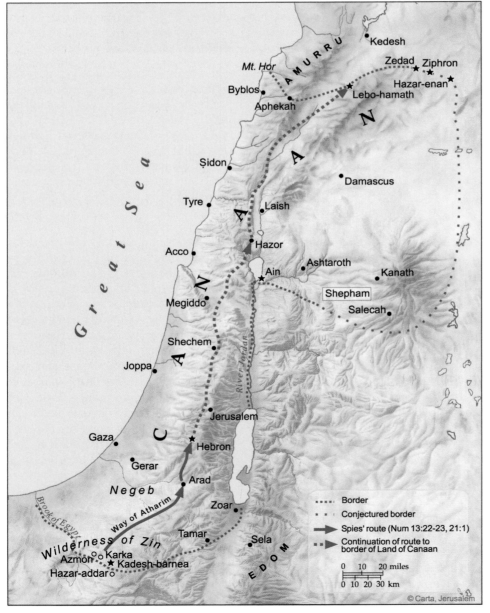

Border
Conjectured border
Spies' route (Num 13:22-23, 21:1)
Continuation of route to border of Land of Canaan

0 10   20 miles
0 10 20 30 km

© Carta, Jerusalem

Outsiders looking in were sometimes of the same opinion. The ancient Egyptians joked about Canaan as "that poor country that has to depend on [the vagaries] of rainfall." Not to be outdone, the Greek geographer Strabo (c. 64 B.C.–A.D. 24) spoke about the high hill country around Jerusalem this way:

> Now Moses…led them away to this place where the settlement of Jerusalem now is, and he easily took possession of the place since it was not a place that would be looked on with envy, nor yet one for which anyone would make a serious fight, for it is rocky and, although it itself is well supplied with water [i.e., by the Gihon spring],

It was a good land….Figs were in it, and grapes. It had more wine than water. Plentiful was its honey, abundant its olives. Every kind of fruit was on its trees. Barley was there, and emmer wheat. There was no limit to any kind of cattle.[9]

its surrounding territory is barren and waterless, and the part of the territory within a radius of sixty stadia [i.e., seven miles] is also rocky beneath the surface.[10]

Sinuhe was a high official from Egypt who fled his homeland (the reasons why are unstated in the story but he seems to have fallen out of favor with the pharaoh) to inland Syria via Byblos on the north Phoenician coast. Historians debate the actual events, but the geographical context of Egypt and the northern, hillier areas of Canaan as portrayed in the tale is entirely realistic. One imagines only "the choice things of heaven, with the dew and from the deep lying beneath" (Deut 33:13) as the defining characteristic of the land that Moses had foreseen would be settled by the tribes of Joseph, "the one distinguished among his brothers" (Deut 33:16).

But at the same time there is much that discourages the view. A discerning traveler today will notice that in places not touched by cultivation or irrigation the land is stony and harsh, and for the long months between the end of the latter rains (late spring) and the onset of the early rains (mid-autumn), much is also barren and of the color of dried sage. The blanket of fresh green—be it barley or wheat, wild grasses or wildflowers—that covers the land in the spring is all too brief, and the thirsty ground from which the orchard trees hang heavy with fruit toward the end of summer quickly becomes both crumbly and hard.

And the authors of the Bible knew it. They were as attuned to their land's propensity for dryness and famine as they were to its wetness and blessing, linking the reality of rain to the even stronger reality of its absence, something that dominates fully half the calendar year:

> *The heaven which is over your head shall be bronze, and the earth which is under your feet iron. The LORD will make the rain of your land powder and dust.*
>
> Deuteronomy 28:23–24
>
> *The wild donkeys stand on the bare heights;*
> *they pant for air like jackals,*
> *Their eyes fail for there is no vegetation.*
>
> Jeremiah 14:6

Strabo may have gotten his history a bit wrong in speaking of Moses rather than Joshua as the conqueror of Canaan, but his overall impression of the land of ancient Israel was rather on-target: from the seacoast in the west where, he added, "the whole of this country from Gaza is barren and sandy," to the Rift Valley in the east where "the country is fiery" (*Geography* xvi.2.32, 44), the land had little to impress this erudite (and thoroughly Hellenized) world traveler from the time of Jesus.

In fact, the land of ancient Israel—the womb from which the descriptions of the biblical writers and their contemporaries have sprung—is a land of both blessing and curse, and in this it is an antinomy. The reasons, we shall see, are partly due to its tremendous geographical dissimilarities, but also to our mistaken tendency to think that the Promised Land deserves to be something consistently better.

Irrigation agriculture in the fields west of Arad, where rainfall averages only 6 inches per year.

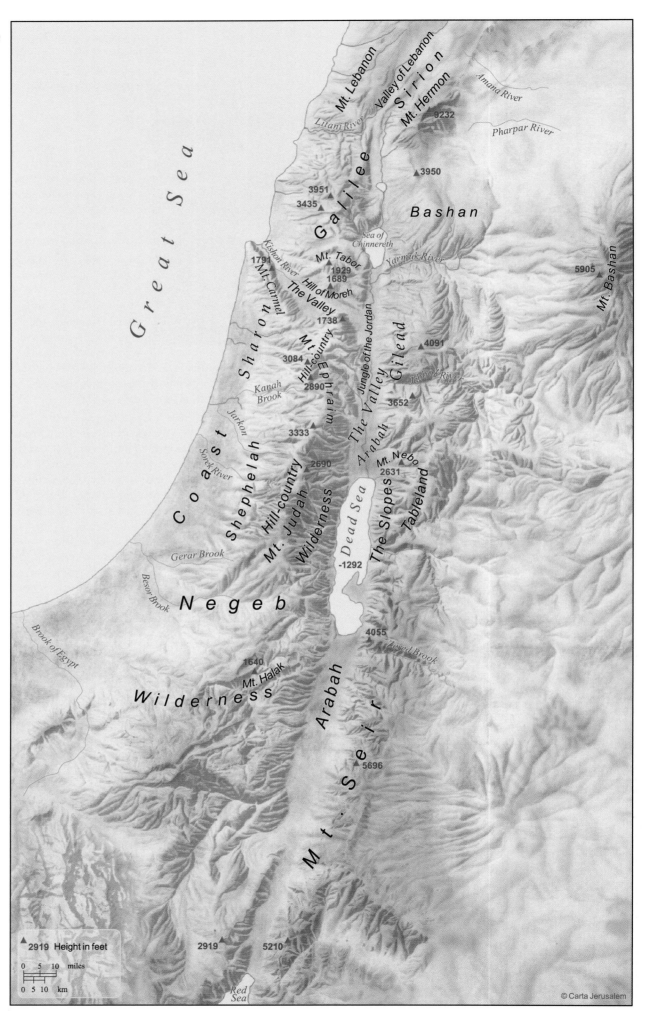

▲ **2919** Height in feet

0   5   10   miles

0 5 10   km

© Carta Jerusalem

C. "A LAND OF HILLS AND VALLEYS THAT DRINKS WATER FROM THE RAIN OF HEAVEN" — DEUTERONOMY 11:11

Speaking practically rather than theologically, a number of factors of geography have conspired to place a highly diverse set of ecosystems within the confines of the land of ancient Israel, which was a pretty small place to begin with, even within the context of the eastern seaboard of the Mediterranean. Nearly all are landforms, natural resources or patterns of climate that can be found in other places on the globe. What is unique here is their confluence in such a tight space. Indeed, the traditional longitudinal dimension of biblical Israel, "from Dan even to Beersheba" (2 Sam 24:2; 1 Kgs 4:25; 2 Chron 30:5), stretched all of 110 miles (177 km), and this was its largest dimension. East to west, we measure thirty miles (48 km) from the port of Acco to the Sea of Galilee, or fifty-five miles (88 km) from Gaza to the Dead Sea; adding the arable land of Transjordan pushes the eastern edge of permanent settlement out another sixty miles (96 km) in the north but only another twenty-five (40 km) in the south. If one speaks instead of the actual heartland of ancient Israel, a place which was confined to the high, hard limestone hill country between Beersheba and the Jezreel Valley, the living space is much smaller—a narrow, rounded hump some twenty-five by seventy miles (40 by 120 km) in size. This, the combined tribal inheritance of Judah, Benjamin, Ephraim and Manasseh, was the area that Judah (in the south) and Israel (in the north) could not afford to lose and still maintain their independence as nation states. It was also the landscape that most easily gave rise to the images that so characterized ancient Israel: vines (Ps 80:8–11); olives (Ps 128:3); springs (Ps 104:10) and grass that quickly withers (Ps 90:5–6).

First among the geographical features that defines the land of ancient Israel is its **topography**. Here we see a tight interplay of hills and valleys, sometimes separated by sharp drops or precipitous cliffs. A simple schematic shows a four-fold division on longitudinal lines: a narrow coastal plain backed by a range of hills (Galilee, Manasseh/Ephraim and Judah) which drop into the Rift Valley and then rise again to the vast Transjordanian Plateau. The main lines generally run north-south, although the coastal plain and hill country angle slightly north-northeastward, with the effect that the uplift that formed the hills side-swipes the Rift Valley just south of the Sea of Galilee. Angular fault lines project from the Rift at various angles, thrusting down-faulted valleys that penetrate the hills in both Cisjordan and Transjordan (the lands of Cisjordan lie west of the Rift; Transjordan encompasses those to the east). The greatest of these down-faulted valleys is the Jezreel Valley, a broad, triangular depression which, together with the wide Harod Valley as its eastward extension, forms a low and easy passage between the coastal plain and the Rift. The Farah Valley, narrower in width and shorter in length, is equally important for peoples living in the interior of the Manasseh hills in that it funnels traffic to the Rift, then points travelers to the highlands of Gilead beyond. East and southeast of the Dead Sea a number of sharp fault lines dissect the scarp that rises to the highlands of Moab and Edom, slicing their western, Judah- and Negev-oriented faces into a jumbled mass that serves to isolate the towns and villages above:

> You who live in the clefts of the rock,
> In the loftiness of your dwelling place....
>
> Obadiah 3

Eastward from the southern end of the coastal plain runs the Negev Basin (Num 13:17), a down-warped depression that channels traffic between the coast and the famed Spice Route of the Arabian Peninsula. Back up in Galilee, a mash of fault lines run mainly

PHYSICAL MAP OF THE ANCIENT NEAR EAST

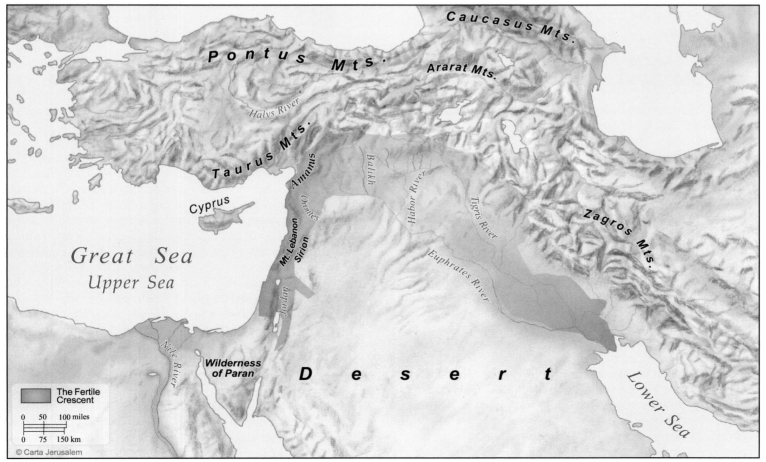

Caucasus Mts.

Pontus Mts.

Ararat Mts.

Halys River

Taurus Mts.

Amanus

Balikh

Habor River

Tigris River

Zagros Mts.

Cyprus

Orontes

Mt. Lebanon

Sirion

Euphrates River

Great Sea

Upper Sea

Jordan

Nile River

Wilderness of Paran

D e s e r t

Lower Sea

The Fertile Crescent

0   50   100 miles

0   75   150 km

© Carta Jerusalem

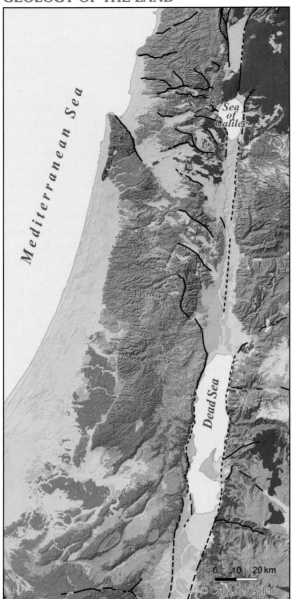

Geological Age			Rock Group		
Cenozoic	Quaternary	Holocene		Dead Sea	Conglomerate Units / Volcanic Units
Cenozoic	Quaternary	Pleistocene	Kurkar	Dead Sea	
Cenozoic	Tertiary	Pliocene	Saqiye	Dead Sea	
Cenozoic	Tertiary	Miocene	Saqiye		
Cenozoic	Tertiary	Oligocene – Upper Eocene			
Cenozoic	Tertiary	Eocene			
Cenozoic	Tertiary	Paleocene – Senonian			
Mesozoic	Cretaceous Upper	Turonian – Cenomanian		Kurnub	Volcanic Units
Mesozoic	Cretaceous Lower	Albian – Neocomian	Arad	Kurnub	
Mesozoic	Jurassic		Arad		
Mesozoic	Triassic		Ramon		
Paleozoic	Ordovician Cambrian		Reed Sea		
Precambrian			Reed Sea		

0 10 20 km

—— Main fault
- - - - Covered fault

©Carta, Jerusalem

east-west, creating broad, fertile valleys just north of the Jezreel Valley (Lower Galilee) but a heavily dissected, closed topography further north where Upper Galilee merges into the soaring Lebanese Range. Throughout the entire land, the topography is dominated by hills—rising, tumbling, rugged, dividing, and creating tight living spaces for plants, animals and peoples alike.

The second geographical feature that directly impacts living conditions in the land of ancient Israel is its **foundation of rock and soil**. The foundation is mixed, as might be expected, though composed mostly of limestone.

- The **limestone** comprising the higher elevations of the hill country of Judah, Ephraim and Manasseh, as well as the hills of Galilee, is mostly of a hard, stratified type called **Cenomanian-Turonian**. This type of limestone provides superior building stones that could be quarried relatively easily with soft iron tools in ancient times. Areas of Cenomanian-Turonian limestone are filled with aquifers that collect and transport rainwater, allowing the water to emerge as springs through small openings in exposed strata. Cenomanian-Turonian limestone also produces rich, clayey **terra rossa** soils that are excellent for orchard crops of summer fruit.
- Broad areas of soft, chalky **Senonian** limestone are found mostly in the drier, eastern and southern areas of the southern

Levant such as the Judean Wilderness, regions south and east of the biblical Negev basin, and on the flats of the Moab and Edom plateaus. Senonian chalk is whitish-to-tan in color, crumbly, does not contain aquifers and doesn't quarry well except to extract lime for plaster. On the positive side, it produces soft, easily plowed **rendzina** soils that are best suited for grain crops.

- A large part of the biblical Negev basin stretching from Gerar through Beer-sheba to Arad, adjacent to areas of Senonian chalk, is filled with a wind-deposited powdery soil called **loess**. Like rendzina soils, loess soils resist water penetration but, when plowed, can be suitable for grain.
- Scattered throughout the southern Levant, though mostly comprising foothills (Heb. *shephelah*) that are somewhat lower than the higher areas of Cenomanian-Turonian limestone, is a relatively soft limestone called **Eocene**. Here springs are weak and the soils, termed **Mediterranean Brown Forest**, are semi-productive, though good for grains. The rocky surface of the Eocene foothills is covered by a hard, grey limey crust called *nari* which supports rough scrub growth, impedes agriculture, and can be quarried into course blocks for building.

Although limestones and their attendant soils dominate most of the land of ancient Israel, other types of rocks and soils can also be found in the region, though usually in outlying areas.

- Much of the northeast, including eastern Galilee, the region of the Sea of Galilee and northern Transjordan, is covered by thick layers of heavy, grey-to-black **basalt**. This is the result of violent seismic activity in the geologic past, after the deposition of the limestone strata. Basaltic areas are often filled with natural water collection cavities that support livestock or wildlife. They are also characterized by boulder-strewn surfaces that provide terrain suitable for grazing though not necessarily for agriculture. On the other hand, vast tracts of flat land on the Golan (Bashan) east of the Sea of Galilee are covered by coarse, **black basaltic soils** in which grain thrives.
- **Sand and sand dunes** dominate much of the Mediterranean coast, the composite material of which originated in North Africa and was pushed ashore by counterclockwise currents in the Mediterranean Sea. Inland, these sand dunes have calcified to form ridges of **kurkar** paralleling the line of the coast. *Kurkar* is a rough kind of sandstone that can be cut into building blocks, thereby providing a local building material for coastal cities that is more durable than mudbrick. When unaltered by human intervention, these kurkar ridges impede the flow of water from the hills into the sea, creating vast areas of swampy, tangled ter-

SOILS OF THE LAND

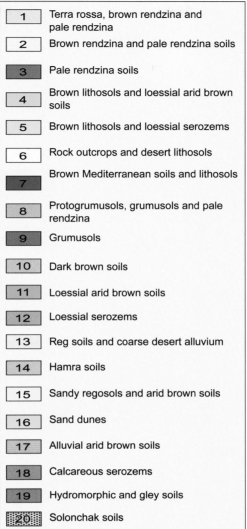

Legend:

1. Terra rossa, brown rendzina and pale rendzina
2. Brown rendzina and pale rendzina soils
3. Pale rendzina soils
4. Brown lithosols and loessial arid brown soils
5. Brown lithosols and loessial serozems
6. Rock outcrops and desert lithosols
7. Brown Mediterranean soils and lithosols
8. Protogrumusols, grumusols and pale rendzina
9. Grumusols
10. Dark brown soils
11. Loessial arid brown soils
12. Loessial serozems
13. Reg soils and coarse desert alluvium
14. Hamra soils
15. Sandy regosols and arid brown soils
16. Sand dunes
17. Alluvial arid brown soils
18. Calcareous serozems
19. Hydromorphic and gley soils
20. Solonchak soils

© Carta, Jerusalem

the higher hills above with the curse of exposed bedrock. The more the rainfall, the greater the amount of soil that is produced from their parent rocks, and the more mature the soils become through the enrichment of cultivation.

Climate, especially rainfall, is the third major factor that impacts living conditions in the southern Levant, and arguably the most important. In a land that lacks a large, perennial river from which water for irrigation can be channeled across an endlessly flat horizon, such as in Egypt and Mesopotamia, the people of ancient Israel were wholly dependent on rainfall:

> For the land into which you are entering to possess is not like the land of Egypt from which you came, where you used to sow your seed and water it with your foot like a vegetable garden. But the land into which you are about to cross to possess it is a land of hills and valleys that drinks water from the rain of heaven.
>
> Deuteronomy 11:10–11

The interface of hills, valleys and the rain of heaven creates four major climactic zones in the Levant:

- A relatively wet **Mediterranean zone**, with fifteen to forty inches (375–1000 mm) of rain annually, concentrated in the winter months, that supports natural woodlands and cultivation year around;
- a dry **Irano-Turanian Steppe zone** in which rainfall rarely exceeds ten inches (250 mm) annually, all of which is restricted to the winter months. Here the landscape is covered with a blanket of green grasses and flowering scrub bushes in the winter and early spring, then reverting to grey-brown for the rest of the year;
- an arid **Sahara-Arabian Desert zone** with rainfall less than four inches (100 mm) annually, most of which is either swallowed up by desert sands (Job 6:15–18) or runs off the powdery soil and;
- a hyper-arid **Sudanese zone**, where rainfall is negligent, highly unpredictable and life is concentrated around scattered oases.

Within these zones rainfall is seasonal, though its effects are most noticeable in the Mediterranean and Irano-Turanian Steppe zones. Rains typically begin in early October. These are the **early rains** (Heb. *yoreh* or *moreh*)—usually soft, sometimes a tempest and always welcome—that break the summer drought, clear the skies of months of built-up haze and soften the ground for plowing:

> The early rain (moreh) covers [the land] with blessings [so that] they go from strength to strength.
>
> Psalm 84:6–7

Then come the **winter rains** of December, January and February (Heb. *geshem* or *matar*) that penetrate the ground, replenish the aquafers, fill the cisterns and create green pastures for grazing. Often these winter rains are violent:

rain. Where drained, the coastal plain is covered either by rich **alluvium**, soils that are washed down from the hill country to the east, or vast swaths of **brown-red sandy soils** composed of a mixture of beach sand and alluvium. Both are extremely fertile, though grains do better in the former and orchard crops, including citrus nowadays, prefer the latter.

- On the far southern and eastern perimeter of the land of ancient Israel, in the Sinai and beyond Edom but also within the cleft of the Rift Valley east and south of the Dead Sea, are areas of white and red **Nubian sandstone**. Exposed mountains of **Pre-Cambrian granite** dominate the southernmost part of the Sinai as well as some of the lowest parts of the Rift, preserving the oldest witness to the geological foundations of the Levant. The soils produced by sandstones and granite are more properly characterized as **desert gravel** and **sand**, material that is largely unproductive for sustained human habitation.

The lines on the ground that differentiate the various types of stone in the southern Levant often can clearly be seen, even by the untrained eye. Distinguishing soil types is a bit more difficult, largely because of the effects of erosion. Water-washed alluvial soils of mixed types fill the broad valleys and plains in the lower elevations, blessing peoples living in the foothills and on the coast with a rich resource for growth while leaving their neighbors in

15

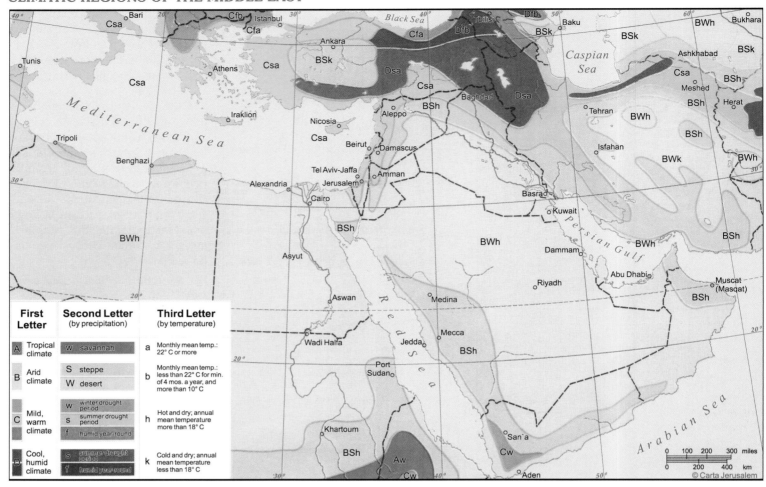

First Letter	Second Letter (by precipitation)	Third Letter (by temperature)
A Tropical climate	w savannah	a Monthly mean temp.: 22° C or more
B Arid climate	S steppe / W desert	b Monthly mean temp.: less than 22° C for min. of 4 mos. a year, and more than 10° C
C Mild, warm climate	w winter drought period / s summer drought period / f humid year-round	h Hot and dry; annual mean temperature more than 18° C
D Cool, humid climate	s summer drought period / f humid year-round	k Cold and dry; annual mean temperature less than 18° C

A flooding rain (geshem) will come,
  and you, O hailstones, will fall,
    and a violent wind will break out.

Ezekiel 13:11; cp. Matt 7:25

Occasionally the winter rains reach even into the expanse of the Sahara-Arabian Desert and Sudanese zones, to places where the entire yearly average can fall in a single downpour:

To bring rain (matar) on a land without people,
  on a desert without a man in it;
to satisfy the waste and desolate land
  and to make the seeds of grass sprout.

Job 38:26–27

Snow (Heb. *sheleg*) falls most winters in the higher elevations (over 2000 feet or 600 meters), a bright, heavy blessing that the writers of the Bible could liken only to an act of God cleansing the soul (Ps 51:7; Isa 1:18). The rains taper off in the spring, usually ending by early May. These **latter rains** (Heb. *malqosh*) swell the heads of grain that blanket fields in hill country and plain alike, the barley first, then the wheat. They coincide with a rise in temperature, prompting an effusion of wildflowers of all possible colors. Although the summer months see virtually no rainfall—"none" would be more accurate—the land is sustained by **dew** (Heb. *tal*) which, at the higher elevations, can account for the equivalent of another seven inches (180 mm) of rain. The effect of dew, dripping off of the leaves of a plant exactly onto the spot of ground where its roots have learned to penetrate deeply into the parched soil, allows orchard trees and vines to produce plump late-summer fruit—olives, figs, pomegranates and vines. Today this menu of crops is bolstered by everything from tomatoes to citrus to kiwi and avocados.

It seems as though all the world admires a warm, sunny day, and that rain gets a bad rap everywhere. This is not biblical. Here, rain is never inconvenient but always a blessing (Matt 5:45), even when cold and soaking wet (Job 24:7–8). That rain is the source of the only substantive supplies of water in the land, and that it comes "from heaven" (Deut 11:11) rather than from one's own clever devices, only heightens the reality of the idea. So, too, is the word of God:

Let my teaching drop as the rain (matar)
  My speech distill as the dew (tal),
as the droplets on the fresh grass,
  and as the showers on the herb.

Deuteronomy 32:2

and:

For as the rain (geshem) and snow come down from heaven
  and do not return there without watering the earth,
making it bear and sprout
  and furnishing seed to the sower and bread to the eater,
so will My word be which goes forth from My mouth.
It will not return to Me empty
  without accomplishing what I desire,
and without succeeding in the matter for which I sent it.

Isaiah 55:10–11

Though always a blessing, rainfall is far from uniform, certainly between the four major climatic zones but also within them. Prevailing rains sweep onto the land from the northwest, off of the Mediterranean Sea, usually as a result of powerful storms in central Europe. As a result, elevations that face west, and/or that are in the north, such as Mount Carmel, the hills of Galilee or the western highlands of Judah, Ephraim and Manasseh, are wetter than those that face deserts that encroach into the land from the south and east (e.g., the Judean Wilderness and the Negev). Higher elevations also tend to be wetter than lower elevations. Patterns of temperature logically follow, with the higher, northern elevations colder than those south and east. Added to these are yearly variations in total rainfall, which can be significant:

> I also withheld the rain from you
>> while there were still three months until harvest,
> I sent rain on one city but no rain on another.
> One field received rain while a field with no rain
>> withered.
> Two or three cities staggered to another city to
>> drink water
>>> but were not satisfied.

Amos 4:7–8

Abraham's initial journey into Canaan forms the template: as soon as he reached the Negev, a place where he eventually would make his home, "there was a famine in the land" (Gen 12:10) that drove him to the better-resourced land of Egypt. But even Egypt is not exempt: Pharaoh's vision of seven fat cows and seven lean cows grazing along the Nile (Gen 41:1–37) speaks of a reality typical to the entire ancient Near East.

The minimum annual rainfall necessary for a farmer to grow wheat and hence be able to sustain permanent settlement is twelve inches (300 mm) per year, with sixteen inches (400 mm) preferred; any less, and anyone seeking to live off the land had best choose a shepherding lifestyle, one that follows seasonal pasturage, instead. Adequate rainfall "in its season" (Deut 11:14) was the great maker and breaker of a life lived on "the good land which the LORD is giving you" (Deut 11:17).

Fourth, the topography, geological foundations and climate of the southern Levant must be seen within **the geographical context of its neighbors**.

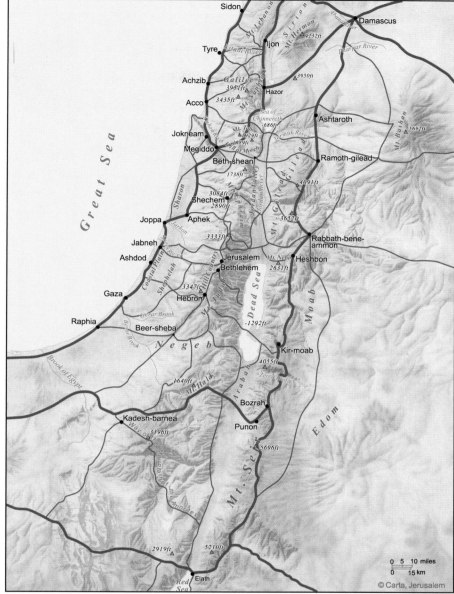

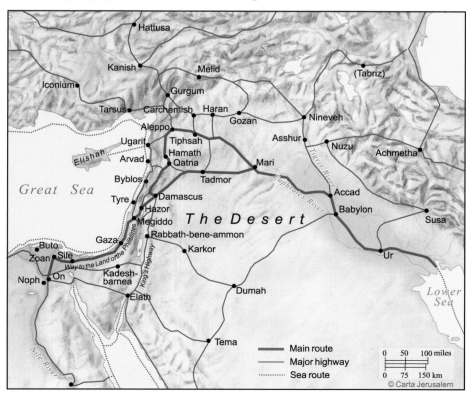

	Main route
	Major highway
	Sea route

Israel is a very narrow land, squeezed between the watery mass of the Mediterranean Sea, the looming hulk of the Lebanese and Anti-Lebanese mountains, and the vast emptiness of the north Arabian and Sinai deserts. The land is too narrow by itself, and too tightly sewn to the land masses Africa, Arabia, Asia and Europe, to temper the priorities of commerce and trade, or the weather patterns, formed beyond its borders. Its history is an endless litany of being overrun, windswept, or oppressed by forces both natural and man-made that lie beyond its control.

The natural features of the southern Levant channel land traffic in what is generally a north-south direction, following the lines of the Mediterranean Sea, the Arabian Desert and the parallel mountainous regions between. East-west traffic is forced to thread its way through gaps in the hills as it makes its way between desert and sea. All in all, the Levant is a busy land bridge, connecting Europe and Asia with Egypt and the Arabian Peninsula, and points beyond.

In our eagerness to track the armies and traders

ROUTES IN THE ANCIENT NEAR EAST

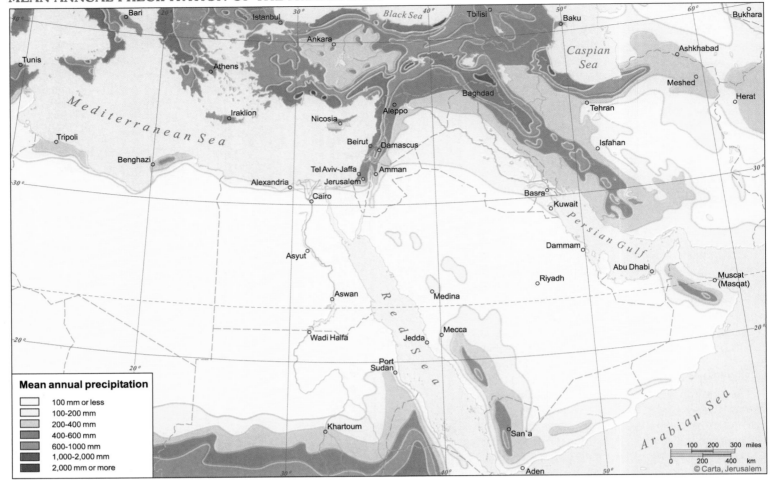

Mean annual precipitation
- 100 mm or less
- 100-200 mm
- 200-400 mm
- 400-600 mm
- 600-1000 mm
- 1,000-2,000 mm
- 2,000 mm or more

© Carta, Jerusalem

of the ancient world along these corridors, we would be remiss if we overlooked the land's role as a migration channel for animals and birds, and a passageway by which plants from one continent have come to flourish in another. Papyrus, for instance, which is native to the Nile Delta, long ago found its way to the Jordan River Valley north of the Sea of Galilee, while pomegranates, a tree so identified with the land of ancient Israel that it is ranked as one of the Seven Species that characterize the land (Deut 8:7–8), is actually native to Persia (Iran) or north India. As for birds, the Levant is as busy a migration corridor between Europe and Africa as are the Straits of Gibraltar at the western outlet of the Mediterranean. The wetness of the Jordan Valley provides a particularly attractive avian passageway, and it is home to a number of migratory bird sanctuaries today. The sudden appearance of quail to the meat-starved masses following Moses out of Egypt may well be an indication of bird migration, aided, as flight often is, by the wind (Ex 16:13; Num 11:31–32; Ps 78:26–29; 105:40). Jeremiah compared the natural rhythm of bird migration with the predictably faithless actions of his people:

Even the stork in the sky knows her seasons;
and the turtledove, the swift and the thrush
observe the time of their migration.
But my people do not know the ordinance of the LORD.

Jeremiah 8:7

Patterns of climate in the Mediterranean basin and in lands beyond Mesopotamia are a great determiner of the living conditions in the compressed Levant between. Even a minor shift in weather patterns abroad causes great fluctuations in the annual Levantine norm. With the onset of winter, a trough of low pressure forms over the eastern Mediterranean Sea, squeezed between high pressure zones lying over the Arabian Peninsula and the Russian steppe

north of the Zagros Mountains. This trough sucks up great amounts of moisture which, when mixed with the warm air of north Africa or Arabia, creates the perfect recipe for storms that track eastward, hitting the Levant with terrifying force before blowing out their energy over the North Arabian Desert:

The voice of the LORD is upon the waters;
the God of glory thunders,
the LORD is over many waters…
The voice of the LORD breaks the cedars,
yes, the LORD shatters the cedars of Lebanon…
The voice of the LORD hews out flames of fire.
The voice of the LORD shakes the wilderness,
the LORD shakes the wilderness of Kadesh…

Psalms 29:3, 5, 7–8

In the summertime, the high-pressure system over the Arabian Desert slides to the northwest, directly over the southern Levant. This minimizes the effects of low pressure systems that tend to hang over India, Iran and Iraq to the east and southern Turkey to the northwest, creating the Levant's well-deserved reputation for oppressive summertime heat.

My strength was drained as in the summer's heat.

Psalm 32:4

Fortunately, for much of the summer, cool Etesian winds blow across the eastern Mediterranean, typically reaching the hills of Judea and Galilee each day by mid-afternoon and continuing until evening. This "cool of the day" (Gen 3:8) tempers the heat produced under the cloudless summertime skies yet provides a stiff enough breeze to winnow the chaff from grain (Hos 13:3).

In the transition seasons between summer and winter, the relative positions of the highs and lows over the Mediterranean Sea, the

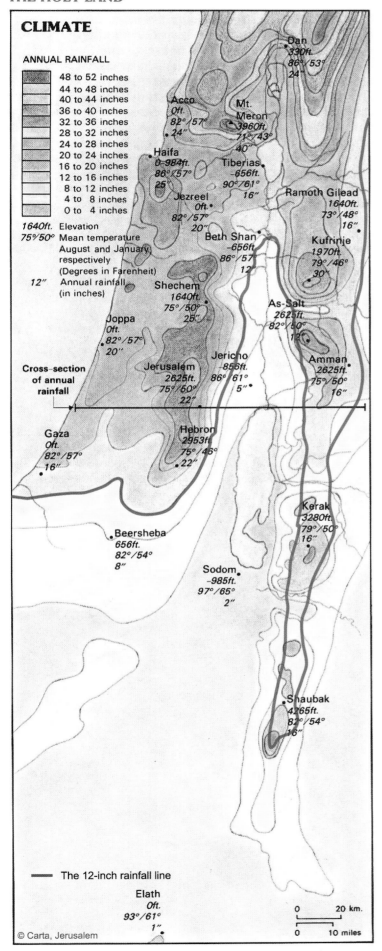

CLIMATE

ANNUAL RAINFALL

- 48 to 52 inches
- 44 to 48 inches
- 40 to 44 inches
- 36 to 40 inches
- 32 to 36 inches
- 28 to 32 inches
- 24 to 28 inches
- 20 to 24 inches
- 16 to 20 inches
- 12 to 16 inches
- 8 to 12 inches
- 4 to 8 inches
- 0 to 4 inches

1640ft. Elevation
75°/50° Mean temperature
August and January
respectively
(Degrees in Farenheit)
12" Annual rainfall
(in inches)

Cross-section
of annual
rainfall

Dan
330ft.
86°/53°
24"

Acco
0ft.
82°/57°
24"

Mt.
Meron
3960ft.
71°/43°
40"

Haifa
0–984ft.
86°/57°
25"

Tiberias
–656ft.
90°/61°
16"

Jezreel
0ft.
82°/57°
20"

Ramoth Gilead
1640ft.
73°/48°
16"

Beth Shan
–656ft.
86°/57°
12"

Kufrinje
1970ft.
79°/46°
30"

Shechem
1640ft.
75°/50°
25"

As-Salt
2625ft.
82°/50°
19"

Joppa
0ft.
82°/57°
20"

Jericho
–856ft.
86°/61°
5"

Jerusalem
2625ft.
75°/50°
22"

Amman
2625ft.
75°/50°
16"

Gaza
0ft.
82°/57°
16"

Hebron
2953ft.
75°/46°
22"

Kerak
3280ft.
79°/50°
16"

Beersheba
656ft.
82°/54°
8"

Sodom
–985ft.
97°/65°
2"

Shaubak
4265ft.
82°/54°
16"

— The 12-inch rainfall line

Elath
0ft.
93°/61°
1"

0   20 km.

0   10 miles

© Carta, Jerusalem

The view eastward from the Herodium. The arable, hard limestone hill country ends exactly where the undulating hills of the Judean Wilderness begin, just past this outlying part of the village of Za'atarah. Here not only does the limestone change from Cenomanian to Senonian, but the shape of the terrain, the quality of the soil, the suitability of the land for crops, and the livelihood of the inhabitants also changes. The foreground is the land of the farmer; the background is the land of the shepherd.

Arabian Peninsula and the Iranian Plateau are not fully established, wreaking havoc on the norm and giving the entire land its well-deserved reputation for climactic unpredictability. The line between blessing and curse is indeed thin, and well known to everyone who makes their living off the lands of the Middle East.

Geographical data such as this provides sets of basic building blocks which, when viewed as holistic systems, allow Bible readers to recognize the many ecosystems that are found in the southern Levant, those in which individual people groups of the Bible lived. What is significant for the biblical narrative is not the variety of ecosystems *per se*, but that so many can be found in such close proximity to each other. A handy comparison would be to try to squeeze the incredible diversity of California into a space as small as New Jersey. Sometimes the transition between one ecosystem and another is sudden, such as that marked by the line between irrigated land and open desert at the edge of the Jericho or En-gedi oases. The north-facing slope of a wadi can be covered with Mediterranean foliage while it's sun-drenched, southern face opposite supports only scrub plants and grasses typical of the Irano-Turanian steppelands. The line where hard Cenomanian limestone ends and soft Senonian chalk begins is dramatically clear in the Judean Desert, with a change not only in surface topography but also groundcover. On the northern Sharon Plain south of Mount Carmel, fields of black alluvial soil lie adjacent to areas of brown-red sands, as clearly defined to the eye as colors are on an artist's palette. The former sprouts grain; the latter orchard crops, typically of citrus. Perhaps most striking is the change found in the canyons that drop off of the high Edomite plateau into the Rift Valley south of the Dead Sea (e.g., the wadis Feifa, Tafila, Khuneizir, Jamal, Dana and Ghuweir), which descend over 6,500 feet (2000 m) in just over ten to thirteen running miles (16 to 21 km). Not only do these wadis expose the full sequence of limestone, sandstone and granite that form the geological foundations of the southern Levant, in doing so they move through all four climatic zones with the appropriate horticulture and zoology of each, every step of the way. More often the shift is gradual, with plant and animal life characteristic of two adjacent ecosystems coexisting in a wide, mixed band. The relevance is in the details, that is, in particular combinations of rock, soil, water resources, elevations and so forth, that form precise environments suitable for specific adaptations to the environment by plants, animals and humans alike.

In spite of the highly variegated nature of the southern Levant, there is a basic division between regions that receive a guaranteed excess of twelve inches (300 mm) inches of rainfall annually and those that don't, that is, a distinction between land where farming predominates and land characterized by shepherding. Generally speaking, while areas that are north, west and high in elevation tend to be wet and those that are south, east and low are dry, two out of three of these criteria are usually enough create an ecosystem that can sustain agriculture. Within this simple twofold classification the land can be subdivided into a few basic types, each with a package of resources that shape specific ecological adaptations. These can be thought of as templates through which a land-traveler or a Bible-reader can form a workable understanding of place. The more common are:

A foothill ecosystem: grain fields in the Elah Valley east of Tel es-Safi (Gath of the Philistines).

A hill country ecosystem: terraces below the village of Battir.

- **Hill country ecosystems** typical of regions designated by the Hebrew word *har*, "mountain" or "hill." Here Cenomanian-Turonian limestone dominates, with deep V-shaped valleys and terraced slopes that retain long, narrow patches of *terra rossa* soil planted with vines and trees of summer fruit. Springs abound, and the hills are usually high enough to catch ample rainfall. Hill country ecosystems are found in the heartlands of Judah, Ephraim, Manasseh, Galilee and Gilead.

Of Joseph [father of Ephraim and Manasseh] he said,
"Blessed of the LORD be his land,
with the choice things of heaven,
with the dew and from the deep lying beneath....
With the best things of the ancient mountains (har)
And the choice things of the everlasting hills..."

Deuteronomy 33:13, 15

- **Foothill ecosystems** typical of regions designated by the Hebrew word *shephelah*, "lowland." These are zones of *nari*-covered Eocene, with low, rolling hills covered in scrub forests and wide, flat valleys filled with alluvium that is suitable for winter-grown grain. Springs are weak, with local water needs compensated by runoff rainfall. Foothill ecosystems are found just west of hill country ecosystems in Judah and Galilee, and north of the hill country of Gilead.

When [Samson] had set fire to the torches he released the foxes into the standing grain of the Philistines [who lived in Timnah, in the foothills], thus burning up both the shocks and the standing grain, along with the vineyards and groves [on the slopes above the valley].

Judges 15:5

- **Broad valley and plain ecosystems** typical of regions designated by the Hebrew words *biq'a*, "broad valley" and, sometimes, *emeq*, "vale," and *mishor*, "level country." These are low, flat, wide areas filled with alluvial soils or soils mixed with sands, where the water table is high and runoff sluggish. The terrain is alternatively swampy or extremely fertile, depending on the season and the slope of the ground, and the main building material mudbrick.

I am a rose of the Sharon [Plain],
a lily of the valleys (emeq).

Song of Songs 2:1

A broad valley ecosystem: the village of Sulam (site of ancient Shunem) enveloped by the fertile fields of the Harod Valley.

A coastland ecosystem: the Mediterranean harbor of Acco, with the rise of Mt. Carmel in the distance.

A tableland ecosystem: the grain fields of Moab, separated by stone boundary markers.

- **Coastland ecosystems** typical of regions designated by the Hebrew words *hof yammim*, "seashore." Coastland ecosystems along the Levantine portion of the Mediterranean are dominated by sand, dunes and protrusions of *kurkar* which either hinder transport and shipping or can be shaped into harbors. Ecosystems bordering the freshwater inland sea (the Sea of Galilee, or the Kinneret) are especially blessed with an abundance of fresh water and alluvial soil. In each instance, ports control shipping and trade, and become centers of fishing.

Asher remained at the seashore (hof yammim)
and stayed in its harbors.

Judges 5:17

- **High plateau or tableland ecosystems** typical of regions designated by the Hebrew word *mishor*, "level country." These regions are found in northern Transjordan (Bashan) and southern Transjordan (Moab and Edom) where the "high is wet" formula trumps "east is dry." Rainfall is adequate to support large tracts of land covered with black basaltic and rendzina soils, both of which are suitable for grain and hence permanent settlement. Tableland ecosystems also support flocks of sheep and goats that graze on summertime stubble.

Then [the tribes of Gad and Reuben] came near to [Moses] and said, "We will build here [on the mishor] *sheepfolds for our livestock and cities for our children."*

Numbers 32:16

A steppe-land ecosystem: a Bedouin encampment, with some modern conveniences, in the hills of eastern Benjamin.

- **Steppe-land ecosystems** typical of regions designated by the Hebrew word *midbar*, "wilderness," or *naveh*, "grazing pastureland." These are areas of rainfall below 12 inches (300 mm) per year. Living conditions are especially compromised when the steppe-land is dominated by a surface topography of Senonian chalk such as in the Judean Wilderness and much of Negev south and east of Beer-sheba. Steppe-land regions are suitable for semi-nomadic herding of sheep and goats, generally forming a wide band between arable lands and open desert.

  The LORD is my shepherd, I shall not want.
  He makes me lie down in grazing pasture-
  *land (*naveh*).*

  Psalm 23:2

- **Desert oasis ecosystems** typical of regions designated by the Hebrew words *'aravah*, "desert-plain," *jeshimon*, "wasteland" and sometimes *midbar* as "uninhabited land." Here rainfall is negligible and population centers are limited to scattered oases. These ecosystems, which encircle the hyper-salty Dead Sea, are also found out on the ragged edges of the southern Levant beyond where even flocks of goats are easily raised. Here the economy is driven by long-distance camel-caravan trade which makes its way to desert ports, the first line of cities traders encounter as they approach tableland or steppe-land zones from the south or east.

  Where is the LORD who brought us up out of the land of Egypt,
  *who led us through the uninhabited land (*midbar*),*

  *through a land of deserts ('*aravah*) and of pits,*
  through a land of drought and of deep darkness,
  through a land that no one crossed
  and where no one dwelt?

  Jeremiah 2:6

We must keep in mind that nearly always the borders between these ecosystems are rather indistinct, with mixed adaptations in the bands between. These seams are important for a number of reasons, though primarily as points of interface for trade and, perhaps more practically on the day to day level of their local residents, because of the possibility to support a mixed diet.

Always eager to consider what makes for skill in living, the writer of Ecclesiasticus reduced the physicality of life to its essence:

The essentials for life are water and bread
and clothing and a house to cover one's nakedness.

Sirach 29:21

He followed up with a list that, fortunately for the ancients, is a bit less Spartan:

Basic to all the needs of a man's life are water and fire and iron and salt
and wheat flour and milk and honey; the blood of the grape, and oil and clothing

Sirach 39:26

By implication, the various ecosystems of the land of the Bible, taken together, offer enough for a life lived in *shalom*, the way it is supposed to be.

A desert oasis ecosystem: the oasis of Moses' Spring in west central Sinai. The stone enclosure is a well.

D. "FROM THE CEDAR THAT IS IN LEBANON EVEN TO THE HYSSOP THAT GROWS ON THE WALL" — 1 KINGS 4:33

It is perhaps time to pause a bit to ask the "but how do we know?" question. How do we identify and classify the plants and animals of the biblical world so that we stand a reasonable chance of filling its ecosystems with life that was really there? "Great are the works of the LORD," declared the Psalmist. "They are sought out [i.e., studied] by all who delight in them" (Ps 111:2). Solomon, we read, did just that,

> with very great discernment and breadth of mind…he spoke of trees, from the cedar that is in Lebanon even to the hyssop that grows on the wall. He spoke also of animals and birds and creeping things and fish.
>
> (1 Kgs 4:29, 33)

Solomon the Naturalist (his naturalism was subsumed under the living God) knew the natural bounty of his realm. The question is, can we?

Our search to identify the plants and animals that inhabited the world of the Bible leads us through three sources of information: geography, texts and archaeology. Meaningful conclusions are drawn first from carefully collecting data, then by organizing the data and cataloging it properly, and finally by observing significant patterns the data may hold. This is no simple task; here, at best we can survey just bits and pieces that are representative of the whole.

First: a look at the **geography** of the lands of the Bible today gives us an overview of ecosystems which, in broad strokes, do indeed represent those of the past. Many of the species that inhabit the southern Levant can be traced back to ancient times. Since the ecosystems that sustain them have been—until quite recently—largely stable, their overall composition can, for the most part, be trusted. And so, for instance, if we look for stands of sycamore trees in the lowlands (1 Kgs 10:27) or oaks on Bashan (Ezek 27:6) we are not disappointed; remnants of very old sycamores on and beyond the outer Shephelah and oaks at Horshat Tal just below Bashan today suggest much larger stands in antiquity. Or, we can inspect the ways of life of the hill country village farmer or the steppe-dwelling Bedouin, whose immediate ancestors have lived off of what is locally available for millennia, and hear distinct echoes of lifestyles of the past. In this part of the world, as with traditional societies everywhere, anthropology intersects nicely with geography.[11]

The tendency, of course, is to look at what is growing on or living in the land today without taking adequate time to distinguish

A sycamore tree, at home in the lower elevations of the Shephelah.

ancient species from ones that are migratory, invasive or have been introduced intentionally. We can debate whether or not each of the seven species (Deut 8:8) is actually native to the land of ancient Israel—they are certainly ancient enough to be considered "biblical"—but citrus, the prickly-pear cactus, the weeping willow, and certain species of mollusks, insects and rodents, to name just a few, are more recent arrivals, including an extravagant variety of garden and decorative plants available in nurseries throughout Israel today. Equally misleading is the tendency to identify plants and animals mentioned in the Bible with species typical to the homeland of the reader. We who read the Bible in European languages are especially prone to this predisposition, bringing images of British or American gardens or lush pastoral meadows to mind. Whatever the rose (Heb. *havatzelet*) of Sharon (Song of Songs 2:1) is—and scholarly suggestions proliferate[12]—it is decidedly not the English rose; that Hebrew word (*vered*) does not appear anywhere in the Bible. Similarly, the sycamore, a popular shade tree in Europe and North America, is not the sycamore of the Bible, a member of the fig family (*Ficus sycomorus*) properly distinguished by spelling its second syllable with an "o" rather than an "a." The hazel, chestnut and hemlock, all of which found their way into the Authorized Version (Gen 30:37; Amos 6:12 KJV) are indeed beautiful trees—in England. Over 2800 species of flowering plants have been classified in modern Israel, as well as 80 species of wild animals (not including reptiles or insects) and nearly 380 species of birds. The question, of course, is how many of these are native so as to begin to match them with terms for plants and animals that occur in ancient texts.

And the **texts** are plentiful. The Bible is our primary written source. We are concerned first with plants and animals that are mentioned in connection with specific ecosystems:

The high mountains are for the wild goats (Heb. ya'el);
the cliffs a refuge for the rock badgers (Heb. shefan).

Psalm 104:18

An ageless Tabor oak at Horshat Tal in northern Galilee.

From the summit of Senir and Hermon,
  from the dens of lions (Heb. 'ari),
  from the mountains of leopards (Heb. namer*).*

Song of Songs 4:8

The king made silver as common as stones in Jerusalem, and he made cedars as plentiful as sycomore trees (Heb. shiqmim*) that are in the lowland.*

1 Kings 10:27

Many of the place names mentioned in the Bible and other ancient sources are also plant names, and it is safe to assume that each place took its name from an animal or plant or resource that actually lived or grew in the area. Examples abound: Socoh ("thorn bush"), Elah ("terebinth"), Aijalon ("deer"), Carmel ("garden land"), Kiriath-jearim ("village of the scrub forest"), Gethsemane ("oil press"), En-rimmon ("spring of the pomegranate"), etc.[13] To these can be added nearly every place name listed in the itinerary of Israel's travels through the Sinai (Num 33:1–49): Hazeroth ("grassy places"), Ritman ("place of the broom trees"), Rimmon-perez ("breaking out of the pomegranates"), Rissah ("moist spot") and so on.

To be proper, we should make catalog listings of all of the plants and animals mentioned in the Bible by their Hebrew, Aramaic and Greek names, together with as much of the context of the natural world as is included in each instance. This has been done elsewhere, with great success.[14]

All in all, there are nearly 180 Hebrew words for animals and 110 words for plants in the Hebrew Bible, a number far less than the number of species that live in the land today. Many of these overlap since the total number of actual species mentioned in the Hebrew Bible, as far as we can tell, is far less: about thirty species of wild animals and another ten that were domesticated. One thing is clear: the ancients classified species differently than we do today, which is part of the problem of sorting the data (more on this below).

In any case, while the biblical data alone is daunting, the task of identifying and cataloging plants and animals of the biblical world becomes quite a bit larger when we consider the wealth of data found in other primary sources. Among these are natural histories of the southern Levant written by Greek and Latin authors such as Herodotus, Strabo, Pliny, Theophrastus and Galen. Each wrote as a dweller of the Mediterranean world, interested primarily in the coastlands lining the sea. They crossed into the hinterland only sporadically, noting in the process places of special interest such as the "delightful stream" of the Jordan or "that gloomy lake, the Dead Sea."[15] Pliny mentions numerous palm groves of Jericho[16] while Strabo notes that the dates of the palms of Tiberias were better than those of the Nile Delta.[17] Back on the coast, he adds that the country around Ascalon (Ashkelon) was a good onion market[18] and that there was a large forest just south of Mount Carmel.[19] All of this is helpful, but the overall impression gained is that classical writers from the Greco-Roman world were not particularly knowledgeable about the far-flung corners of their empire and so mentioned specifics only incidentally, or if they were unusual.

More helpful is Josephus, born in Jerusalem but especially fond of Galilee, the territory that he was charged to defend in the Great Revolt against Rome (A.D. 66–67). Josephus filled his flowing narratives with lengthy asides in which he described the physical layout of strategic cities or the glorious natural bounty of his beloved Galilee. For instance, in the middle of a dramatic description of the bloody battle at Taricheae on the northwestern shore of the Sea of Galilee (the lake of Gennesar) Josephus paused to expound on the bounties of the lake:

> Its water is sweet to the taste and excellent to drink . . . the lake contains species of fish different, both in taste and appearance, from

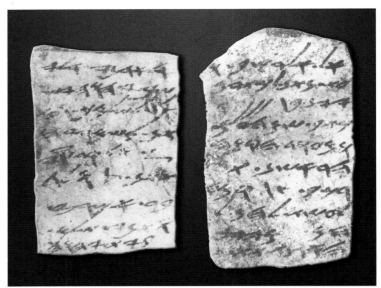

Ostraca from Eliashib's archives; the one on the left mentions "the house of YHWH" (Carta collection).

> those found elsewhere....Skirting the lake of Gennesar lies a region whose natural properties and beauty are very remarkable. There is not a plant which its fertile soil refuses to produce, and its cultivators in fact grow every species; the air is so well tempered that it suits the most opposite varieties. The walnut, a tree which delights in the most wintry climate, here grows luxuriantly beside palm trees, which thrive on heat, and figs and olives which require a milder atmosphere.... Besides being favored by its genial air, the country is watered by a highly fertilizing spring called by its inhabitants Capernaum.[20]

While we might argue to what extent Josephus exercised literary license in exaggerating Galilee's beauty to portray more strongly the shock of its devastation by Rome, we must also take at face value his intimate association with the rich nature of the place.

Equally insightful are the accounts of ancient Egyptian travelers in the land who appropriated its bounty either by trade or by conquest. In addition to the 18th century B.C. account of Sinuhe cited above, we have, for instance, a hypothetical (though very realistic) narrative of the trials of a traveler who had to make his way alone through the unfriendly confines of Canaan, as recorded in the 13th century B.C. Papyrus Anastasi I:

> ...Thou hast [not] trodden the road to [the Magur] where the sky is darkened by day and it is overgrown with cypresses and oaks and cedars which reach the heavens. Lions are more numerous than leopards or hyenas, (and it is) surrounded by Shasu [Bedouin] on (every) side of it....Thy path is filled with boulders and pebbles, without a toe hold for passing by, overgrown with reeds, thorns, brambles and "wolf's paw." The ravine is on one side of thee, and the mountain rises on the other."[21]

Supporting data can be found in lists of plunder taken by conquering pharaohs of Egypt's Eighteenth and Nineteenth Dynasties (15th through 12th centuries B.C.). The scribes of Thutmose III recorded their monarch's conquest of Arvad on the north Phoenician coast in c. 1461 B.C. this way:

> Behold, his majesty overthrew the city of Arvad with its grain, cutting down all its pleasant trees...their gardens were filled with their fruit, their wines were found remaining in their presses as water flows, their grain on the terraces [upon ---] was more plentiful than the sand of the shore. The army were overwhelmed with their portions.[22]

While much of the language in these texts is likely formulaic and the spoils taken surely represent the more valuable of the commodities to be had, a compilation of goods hauled back to Egypt shows that grain, wine and livestock were indeed plentiful in Canaan, perhaps of a quality better than that which could be found back in the land of the pharaohs.[23]

Although the southern Levant is not particularly rich in written sources from the time of the Bible when compared to what has been found in Mesopotamia, Egypt or the Greco-Roman world, a growing collection of texts from ancient Israel has been uncovered by the spade of the archaeologist. These are mostly of the everyday sort, notations written on potsherds or, less frequently, parchment, or inscribed on stone as either burial notices, social or economic notations, or notations indicating weights and measures.[24] Taken as a whole they never intended to tell us, residents of a later inquiring generation, anything, but rather reflect the minutia of everyday life as it was relevant for real living situations in the past. And this is precisely what makes them so valuable. We have, for example, notations of the movement of wine, bread and vinegar from the Israelite fortress at Arad to some undesignated place in the late seventh century B.C.; the mention of harvest and stored grain by a Judean living at Mesad Hashavyahu on the Mediterranean coast in the late seventh century B.C.; detailed notations of the movement of "aged wine" and "purified oil" from landed estates in the hill country of Manasseh to the capital city Samaria in the eighth century B.C.; the transfer of gum, grain, cattle, wine and hay to the Ammonite king in the late seventh or early sixth centuries B.C.; and a calendar from tenth century B.C. Gezer that indicates which agricultural activities took place in which months of the annual cycle. Such documents are important in helping us reconstruct social and economic relationships within the many ecosystems of ancient Israel, as well as the interrelationships between them.

A very different kind of text from the southern Levant sheds light on the normal interrelationship between animal species, mentioning a number of animals, mostly birds, that are at home in the region in the process. This is the Balaam inscription from Deir 'Alla, a large site at the mouth of the Jabbok River in the mid-Jordan Valley. The text, which is written in Old Aramaic and dates, most likely, to the eighth century B.C., contains a vision of Balaam son of Beor (cf. Num 22:5, 20) in which the natural order of the world is turned upside down: "the swallow reproaches the hawk and the owl retorts to the carrion vultures . . . [and the] hyenas give heed to chastisement," etc.[25]

Much relevant information about the ecology of the lands of the Bible can also be gleaned from the Mishnah, Talmud and Patristic writers, including Eusebius and Jerome who lived in Late Roman Palestine in the fourth century A.D. These are all secondary primary sources in that they are, for the most part, commenting on the Bible and its world through their own, later contexts. By and large the mention of ecological data in such sources can be trusted, though each instance needs to be pried away from its halachic or didactic use and seen as a witness to the land in its own right. Of course these post-biblical writers had every right to use the land as a metaphor or an apologetic tool; they were simply following the lead set by the writers of the Bible themselves. The progressive understanding of the ecology of the Bible as it was seen through the eyes of its commentators, that is, the development of a theology of the land, is critical to the process, but lies beyond the scope of this rather introductory study.

We would be remiss not to mention as well a host of pre- and early modern explorers of Ottoman Turkish Palestine who were interested not so much in the holiness of the landscape as in its natural features. Among these are students of the Swedish botanist Carolus Linnaeus, and the Swiss explorer Edmond Boissier who wrote a five volume work on the flora of the Middle East.[26] Of importance as well is the volume on flora and fauna published by the Survey of Western Palestine in 1885,[27] and Gustaf Dalman's magisterial Work and Customs in Palestine that records intimate details of the

Hebrew ostracon from Mesad Hashavyahu: letter of a worker employed in the harvest who complains that his garment was confiscated; he begs the governor to return his property (Carta collection).

Samaria ostracon 1, mentioning the movement of a jar of aged wine from Beerayim to Samaria (Aḥituv, Echoes from the Past, 262).

The so-called "barley ostracon" from Samaria, eighth century B.C. (Aḥituv, Echoes from the Past, 311).

natural world of pre-industrialized Palestine (1928).[28] These works and others of this type are anthropological rather than strictly scientific in nature, yet provide a sensitive, encyclopedic understanding of the plant and animal life of the southern Levant that is largely consistent with that of the biblical periods.

A third source of information is **archaeology**. Here we have an ever-expanding collection of data that can tell us what plants and animals were actually present at particular times and in particular places in the land of ancient Israel, and how they (or products derived therefrom) were used by its ancient inhabitants. Perhaps most obvious are the remains of plants and animals found in excavations. Nearly every kind of seed, pit, husk, stem, hull or even pollen from plants grown in ancient Israel, both domesticated and wild, is able to be recovered and analyzed today, thanks to incredible advances in diagnostic equipment housed in archaeological laboratories. So is the calcified excrement of animals and humans, which contains not only remains of ancient meals but evidence of parasites or worms that infected the eaters' digestive systems. Microscopic examination of potsherds can reveal the kinds of commodities that were once contained in the vessels from which the sherds came. Remains of bones are found in nearly every excavation, providing evidence either of what was eaten, what was sacrificed, or both. Sheep, goat and cattle bones are those most commonly found, although the bones of any animal, including birds and rodents, are fair game for the archaeologist. The presence or absence of pig bones can tell us something about the ethnicity (or at least the religious scruples) of a site's inhabitants: the Philistines tended to be pork eaters, the Judeans not at all and the Northern Kingdom Israelites yes, but not before the mid-eighth century B.C.[29] Even fish bones, as fragile as they are, have been found; a prime example is eighth century B.C. Jerusalem in which were found thousands of bones of fish from both the Mediterranean Sea and the Nile.[30] We note that Jerusalem had a Fish Gate (2 Chron 33:14; Zeph 1:10) and, by implication, a fish market as well, providing a nice juxtaposition of archaeological and textual data that gives evidence for extensive networks of supply, processing and trade between vastly differing ecosystems in the southern Levant.

Equally important are the excavated remains of a host of everyday objects that attest to ways of human adaptation in specific ancient ecosystems. These include agricultural implements and installations such as plow shares, hoes and terraces; systems to store and transport water for irrigation; presses for extracting juice from grapes or oil from olives; sickles, threshing floors, the sharp teeth of threshing sledges, watch towers, silos, storage jars and the like.[31] Fibers of linen and wool from clothing or wraps, and even the leather of sandals—manufactured products that attest to their organic source—are sometimes found in sites along the Dead Sea

Reliefs of pomegranates found in the "botanical garden room" of the Karnak Temple in ancient Thebes, Egypt, carved by artisans of Thutmose III after his conquest of Canaan.

where the lack of humidity slows the processes of decomposition.

Ancient objects of art depicting items or activities of everyday life are also invaluable for reconstructing the ecology of the biblical world. Like texts, these are representations of the past and so must be treated with the same kind of interpretive care that we give to written sources. Is art, even that showing everyday living conditions, realistic, representational or idealistic? And are the objects depicted native, or imported? After pharaoh Thutmose III conquered the southern Levant in the mid-fifteenth century B.C., he had his artisans decorate the inner sanctum of the great Amun-Re temple in Karnak, Egypt, (modern Luxor) with reliefs of exotic plant and animal life that he had seen on his foreign travels. Depicted are pomegranates, a type of iris, gazelles, geese, turtledoves, ravens, marsh birds, an eagle, a lapwing, a plover, a gull and a number of birds not easily identified, though all apparently were native to the southern Levant.[32] The conquering Assyrian king Sennacherib depicted fig trees, grape vines and grain on his relief of the siege and conquest of Lachish which took place in 701 B.C., an indication that summer fruit that we might normally otherwise identify with the Judean hill country was also grown in its outer Shephelah.

Objects of art from Judah or Israel are rare from the time of the Bible, although those that we do have tend to favor floral motifs. The Proto-Aeolic (Proto-Ionic) capitals which decorated palaces in Jerusalem, Ramat Rahel (its ancient name is unknown), Samaria,

A basalt grain mill from the time of the New Testament among the ruins of the site of Gamla.

A Proto-Ionic capital which decorated top of a column in a seventh century B.C. Judean palace in Ramat Rachel, half way between Jerusalem and Bethlehem. The capital depicts the unfolding of palm fronds.

Megiddo, Hazor, and the Ammonite capital Rabbah were intended to represent in stone the unfolding fronds of a palm tree.[33] Royal seal impressions in the seventh century B.C. depicted simple rosettes, a stylized depiction of an open flower, while those of the late eighth century B.C. depicted two-winged sun discs and four-winged beetles, these latter apparently under Egyptian influence.[34] Artisans in Egypt and Mesopotamia were much freer in depicting everyday life scenes than were their colleagues from ancient Israel, and included in their work a wide variety of plant and animal life native to those parts of the world. As the prohibition against graven images relaxed in Late Roman Palestine, equally rich scenes were depicted in mosaics or in stone relief on lintels or sarcophagi in both Christian and Jewish contexts. In the international world of fourth through sixth centuries A.D., mosaic artists imported animal designs from across the known world, even sometimes creating species that lived only in the world of artistic license. While this says more about socio-economic processes than it does local ecology, it nevertheless sets a context in which the ancient inhabitants of the southern Levant were acutely aware of the living world around them.

* * * * *

Dio Cassius, writing in the early third century A.D. (History, XLIII.23.1–2), spoke of a strange animal from north Africa that looked like the hybrid of a camel and a leopard. Having never actually seen a giraffe, people back home imagined the animal exactly as it was described to them. This mosaic depiction of a "camel-leopard," dating to the sixth century A.D., is found in the diaconicon-baptistery of the Moses Memorial church at Siyagha, Mt. Nebo, Jordan. Carl Linnaeus codified the concept by labeling a species of giraffe, now extinct in the northern Sahara, as Giraffa camelopardalis.

Our sources of information are rich. Geography can set the parameters of what can and cannot live within individual ecosystems. Archaeology can tell us what actually did live there. More problematic is to match names found in the texts with actual plants and animals on the ground. As already noted, the ancients did not classify the living things of their world with the same scientific categories that we do in ours, but used more practical criteria instead: old or young, male or female, big or small, their usefulness for humans, or their methods of locomotion. The first chapter of Genesis provides the basic categories, with plenty of allowance for subdivisions "after their kind" as might become practical later on:

> The earth brought forth vegetation, plants yielding seed after their kind, and trees bearing fruit with seed in them, after their kind.
>
> Genesis 1:12
>
> God created the great sea monsters and everything living creature that moves with which the waters swarmed after their kind, and every winged bird after its kind.
>
> Genesis 1:21

> God made the beasts of the earth after their kind, and the cattle after their kind, and everything that creeps on the ground after its kind.
>
> Genesis 1:25.

Compare this to the specialization of Isaiah. The prophet's discourse on agriculture betrays his first-hand knowledge of the subject as it was practiced in eighth century B.C. Judah, with practical, rather than scientific, classification in mind:

> Does the farmer plow continually to plant seed?
>   Does he continually turn and harrow the ground?
> Does he not level its surface
>   and sow dill and scatter cumin
> and plant wheat in rows,
>   barley in its place and rye within its area? …
> For dill is not threshed with a threshing sledge,
>   nor is the cartwheel driven over cumin,
> but dill is beaten out with a rod
>   and cumin with a club.
> Grain for bread is crushed,
>   indeed, he does not continue to thresh it forever.
> Because the wheel of his cart and his horses eventually damage it
>   he does not thresh it longer.
>
> Isaiah 28:24–28

Isaiah knew his stuff, but for us, problems of specific identification abound. One is that there are far more species of flora and fauna that are known to have lived in ancient Israel than there are names preserved in the sources for them. But more than this: a single name in the Bible can also refer to more than one animal or more than one plant. For instance, the Hebrew word 'erez usually refers to the famed cedar of Lebanon (e.g., Judg 9:15; 1 Kgs 5:6; Isa 41:19), but must indicate another kind of tree, shaped similarly and with aromatic wood such as the tamarisk or juniper, when it occurs in contexts of the Sinai (e.g., Lev 14:4–6, 49–52; Num 19:6). The word suf seems to cover a variety of reedy water plants, including several species of reeds, rushes and sea weeds, rather than a specific species. When it occurs in the context of the Nile, reeds or cattails are most likely in mind (e.g., Ex 2:3–5; Isa 19:6). Plants and animals that are neither helpful nor harmful for human activity are the most difficult to identify, partly because there are so many of them and partly because when the Bible does mention them, it is usually in a rather generic manner.

It is much easier to identify words for domestic livestock or for field and orchard crops, as well as for organisms that were harmful to human life, precisely because they played an active role in human affairs. In these cases, rather than having one word for several species we sometimes find several words for one. A good example is "small cattle," varieties of sheep, lambs, rams and goats. We find fourteen words in the Hebrew Bible (two are Aramaic) and another five in the Greek New Testament referring to sheep, distinguishing male from female, young from old, individuals from a flock, and animals for normal use from those intended for sacrifice: 'ayil ("ram," Gen 22:13), keves ("lamb," Ex 29:38), kesev (also "lamb;" the word transposes the consonants, Gen 30:32), kar ("lamb," "ram," 2 Kgs 3:4), rahel ("ewe," Gen 31:38), tzon ("flock," Gen 30:31), seh ("flock," Isa 53:7) and 'eder ("flock," Isa 40:11)—these three can also refer to goats—taleh ("lamb," Isa 40:11), 'ul ("ewe with suckling lamb," Ps 78:71), zemer ("mountain sheep," Deut 14:5), yovel ("ram," Josh 6:5), dekar ("ram," Ezra 6:9), 'immerin ("lamb," Ezra 6:9), probaton ("sheep," Matt 12:11), amnos ("lamb," Jn 1:29), arnion ("lamb," Rev 5:6), aren ("lamb," Lk 10:3) and pascha (the "Paschal" or "Passover lamb," Mk 14:12). This is surely an indication of how important sheep were to the economy of ancient Israel (note the cliché that the Inuit have 300 words for snow). It also tells us that animals (and certainly plants) were classified in the

The lion of the Babylonian goddess Ishtar as depicted on the façade of the Processional Way, leading visitors into Nebuchadnezzar's palace in Babylon; now at the Pergamum Museum, Berlin. Lions represented the strength and virility of the Assyrian and Babylonian kings; in Judah, they were both revered and feared.

ancient world in terms of visible characteristics or practical use rather than by tight scientific criteria as today. Similarly, we have six words for lion in the Hebrew Bible: *'ari* ("male lion"), *'aryeh* ("female lion"), *k'fir* ("young lion"), *lavi'* ("old lion"), *layish* ("strong lion") and *shahal* ("fierce lion"); Job 4:10–11 lists five of the six. As a shepherd boy who watched over his flocks in the wild hills east of Bethlehem, the young David knew his sheep by characteristic and by type, but would also have known all shapes and sizes of lions that crawled up out of the Jordan Valley looking for a quick snack.

Another example: the Bible gives twenty different names for thistles and thorns, but over sixty species of such are known to grow in the southern Levant today. Even allowing for the introduction of some species and the extinction of others, the data cannot be made to match. But how can we even begin to match name to species, especially when the ancients didn't always use our differentiation of species as their determiner of names?

Let's start with a quick analogy. The location of many place names from the time of the Bible are known today because they were passed down from Hebrew or Greek to Arabic. So the Hebrew name of the biblical city Michmash is preserved in Arabic today as the village of Mukmas, and the Greek name Neapolis has become the Arabic Nablus, and so on. So, too, there are many plant and animal names in biblical Hebrew that have been preserved in Mishnaic (post-New Testament) Hebrew, Aramaic, Syriac and/or Arabic. We must remember that in the centuries between the fall of the Temple to Rome in A.D. 70 and the beginning of the large-scale return of the Jews to the land in the late nineteenth century A.D., Palestina/Palestine was inhabited by a mass of small-scale village farmers who were beholden to the land off of which they eked out a living. In spite of long-term political takeovers of the land by outside powers, living conditions on the ground remained relatively stable, preserving ancient patterns of livelihood and ecology across the millennia. Local populations continued to speak their native Semitic dialects in spite of the imposition of imperial languages by the ruling elite. They continued to call the minutia of their daily lives by the same or similar terms that their ancestors did and that their descendants would. In this way, a good many Hebrew, Aramaic and Syriac terms for plants, animals and other ecological features came over into Arabic after the Islamic conquest of the seventh century A.D. Via Arabic, many have been preserved until today, though with understandable linguistic changes over time. This is particularly helpful for terms that are otherwise rare in the Hebrew Bible. Examples are Arabic *butm* for Hebrew *botnim*, "pistachio nuts" (only in Gen 43:11); Arabic *lauz* for Hebrew *luz*, "almond tree" (only in Gen 30:37); Arabic *tuffah* for Hebrew *tappuah*, "apple" (Prov 25:11; Song of Songs 2:3; 7:8; 8:5; Joel 1:12) and Arabic *laith* for Hebrew *layish*, "strong lion" (Job 4:10; Prov 30:30; Isa 30:6).[35]

Other plants or animals can be identified, at least tentatively, through known Semitic roots. English translations render both *ḥeppor-perot* (Isa 2:20) and *ḥoled* (Lev 11:29) as "mole." Both roots, *ḥpr* (biblical Hebrew) and *ḥld* (Mishnaic Hebrew), mean "to dig," which suggests the same semantic range of meaning for both. The geographical context helps: the common mole (*Talpa europaea*)

is never found in Israel, though the Mole Rat (*Spalax ehrenbergi*), a look-alike, is. In any case, we are left to speculate whether these are two terms for the same animal, or if two similar animals are intended. Both words occur only once in the Hebrew Bible, so their literary context is thin. Of course all proposed identifications need to take into account both geographical and literary contexts, and it is here that debates as to proper identification can be sharp. We recall that it is geographical context that determines when *erez* must mean juniper and not cedar, or when *suf* refers to cattails in particular, rather than reeds generically.

When a proper identification of a plant or animal cannot be known, one solution is to leave the name untranslated so as to puzzle readers and non-readers of Hebrew and Greek alike. What is the *behemoth* (Job 40:15), a term that linguistically is an intensification of the Hebrew term *behemah*, "beast"? Untranslated, the word has entered English to refer to something of monstrous size or power. Suggestions for the *behemoth* of Job include the elephant, the crocodile or, most frequently, the hippopotamus, based on its literary description (Job 40:15–24), though each of these options stretches the geographical borders of the book. So, too, *leviathan*, the greatest of the creatures of the sea (Job 41:1; Ps 74:14; 104:26; Isa 27:1). Literary critics are quick to draw parallels to mythical creatures that were thought to inhabit the watery edges of the earth, or were subdued in the Babylonian creation epic. Naturalists prefer the Nile crocodile, tame by comparison, although again the reader is left to wonder how wide the intended geographical scope of the biblical writers actually was. With terms such as these, the lack of a translation might actually be the best translation.

With these principles of identification and cautions of research in mind, we can turn briefly to some lists. Most of the plants and animals mentioned in the Bible fall, quite understandably, into two categories: those that are helpful to people, and those that are harmful.

Helpful creatures are those that supply food[36] (the milk or meat of animals; fruit, grain or other edible parts such as leaves of plants), those that supply products that can be used for clothing, shelter or tools, and those that can be used as beasts of burden. A conventional list of plants itemizes the so-called **seven species**, a collection of flora that typifies the varied ecosystems of the land of ancient Israel and together provided the Israelite a yearlong diet of staples and sweets. Though itemized in Deuteronomy 8:8, these seven species appear in various combinations throughout all genres of the biblical story. They reference actual foodstuffs grown but also signify certain characteristics of God, the land and his people.

- **Wheat** (Heb. *hittah*). Wheat is the main ingredient in bread, the staff of life and mainstay of every meal (Matt 6:11). The grain farmer needs a minimum of twelve inches of rainfall each winter to raise wheat, making that climatological line on the ground the marker dividing the land where farming and hence permanent village life is possible from that where shepherding dominates. While the best fields for wheat are found in the broader valleys of the lowlands and the Galilee, on the Transjordanian tablelands and on the coast, enough wheat can be grown in the hill country to enable villages that lie everywhere within the twelve-inch line to be largely self-sufficient in the basics of life. Wheat, along with olive oil, was ancient Israel's most valuable trade export (1 Kgs 5:11; Ezek 27:17; cf. Acts 12:20), and its absence was a sure indication of famine. Wheat's poorer cousin, emmer (Heb. *kussemet*), is mentioned only three times in the Hebrew Bible (Ex 9:32; Isa 28:25; Ezek 4:9) though it is one of the most ancient varieties of grain domesticated in the ancient Near East.

Wheat in the Beth Netopha Valley, Lower Galilee.

- **Barley** (Heb. *se'orah*, lit. "bearded grain"). This grain, which needs only eight inches of rain to mature, is especially suited for the hotter, dryer steppe regions in which livestock predominates. Barley is less-expensive (Rev 6:6) and rougher than wheat, with high dietary fiber, and produces a kind of course bread that was the fare of the poorer, common folk of ancient Israel (Judg 7:13; Ezek 4:9–12; cf. Hos 3:2). It was, in fact, considered mostly to be food for livestock. Barley ripens about a month earlier than wheat (Ex 9:31–32; cf. Ruth 1:22). The time between the beginning of the barley harvest and the end of the

Barley below the Shawbak castle in the highlands of Edom.

wheat harvest (i.e., from the Feast of Unleavened Bread to the Feast of Harvest "of the first fruits of your labors from what you sow in the field" Ex 23:15–16) was normally about six to eight weeks.

Grapes typical to the hill country of Judah and Ephraim.

- **Vine** (Heb. *gefen*; with *'enav*, grape, *'eshkol*, grape cluster and *kerem*, vineyard). While wheat may have been the dietary staple in the ancient Near East, grapes are the foodstuff most characteristic of ancient Israel. With healthy water a rare commodity nearly everywhere, the Egyptians and Babylonians drank barley beer; Israel drank wine. Like other orchard crops of summer fruit, grape vines are especially suited for the higher-elevated, hard limestone hills of the southern Levant that form the heartlands of Judah (Gen 49:10–12), the Joseph tribes (Ephraim and Manasseh; Gen 49:22), and Gad, the dominant Israelite tribe in Transjordan (Gilead). Noah's first planting was a vineyard (Gen 9:20), and the twelve spies were especially keen to bring back to Moses an especially large grape cluster from the valley of Eshkol (the Valley of the Grape Cluster; Num 13:20–23) high in the Hebron hills. The vine became the definitive symbol of ancient Israel, a people as choice as the fruit (Ps 80:8–19; Isa 5:1–7; Jer 2:21; Ezek 19:10–11; Amos 9:13; Jn 15:1–6; Rev 14:18–20).

Figs in Bethlehem in the hill country of Judah.

- **Fig tree** (Heb. *t'enah*; when plural, *t'enim*, the word can also refer to the figs themselves). The first fruit mentioned by name in the Bible (Gen 3:7), the fig tree is most at home in the same high limestone hill country as is the vine. As such, in the biblical writer's mind the fig became pared with the vine to form the ideal environment in which Israel could live in security and peace (Num 13:23; 1 Kgs 4:25; 2 Kgs 18:31; Mic 4:4; Zech 3:10). The fig tree is as striking in winter as it is in the summer. During winter, its light grey branches rattle about with the appearance of old bones;[37] in the summer, it produces large,

Pomegranate in Jerusalem in the hill country of Judah.

richly-greened leaves. The fig tree gives fruit twice each year: the early, springtime fruit, Gk. *pagae* (Hos 9:10; Lk 21:29–30), is hardly edible; if it doesn't form (Matt 21:18–21) neither will the late summer figs. These later figs are especially sweet and can be preserved as dried, pressed cakes (1 Sam 25:18; 30:12).

- **Pomegranate** (Heb. *rimmon*). The bush-like leaves of a pomegranate tree are by nature small, curled and nondescript, but the fruit is especially bold: large, yellowish-red, decorated with a six-pointed crown and bursting with juicy seeds. So too the fragrant late-spring flower, with elongated, bell-shaped petals of crimson-orange. The fruit is usually eaten as a garnish rather than a meal, with a taste that is sweet though with a bitter edge. Its juice makes for spiced wine (Song of Songs 8:2). Of all of the hill country summer fruit, it is the beauty of the pomegranate that most readily came to symbolize love between persons (cf. Song of Songs 4:3, 13; 6:7, 11) or that of the priesthood for the temple (Ex 28:33–34; 39:24–26; 1 Kgs 7:18, 20; 2 Chron 3:16; 4:13). The popular notion that each pomegranate contains the same number of seeds as there are commandments in the Torah (613) expands that symbolism to include the love of God for his Torah. Alternately, throughout the ancient Near East the mass of seeds in the pomegranate gave rise to notions of fertility.

- **Olive oil** (Heb. *zeit shemen*; with *zayit*, olive). Like the vine, fig tree and pomegranate, the olive tree is most ably suited to the high hill country of the southern Levant. But the olive can also thrive where the soil is rocky and poor (Mark Twain once called the olive "the fast friend of worthless soil"[38]). Because the olive tree is evergreen (it never loses all of its leaves at once), its leafy presence stands as a sentinel of blessing even in the harshest of growing conditions. The tree grows slowly, with thick, gnarled trunks hundreds of years old still able to produce fresh shoots. As such, it, perhaps more than any other plant of the biblical world, offers images of steadfast certainty and blessing (Ps 128:3). The fruit is primarily used for oil, for food (it actually combats cholesterol), for cooking, for lamp fuel, for medicine, as solvents for incense and perfume, and for anointing kings and priests.

Olives in Jerusalem in the hill country of Judah.

- **Honey** (Heb. *davash*). Western logic might suggest that the seventh specie is the sweet, sticky product of the bee (Heb. *devorah*), and bees certainly were a part of the biblical world (Deut 1:44; Judg 14:8; Ps 118:12; Isa 7:18).[39] But the context here suggests that honey should be a derivative of a plant rather than the product of an insect, and so commentators generally agree that the referent is the distilled paste of dates. Semitic languages use cognates of the Hebrew word *davash* for date paste (e.g., *dishpu* in Akkadian, *dibs* in Arabic), with the Jerusalem Talmud (*Bikkurim* 1,3) giving the summary opinion: "And honey—it is dates." The date palm (Heb. *tamar*) needs plenty of sun for its fruit to ripen and ample groundwater to which its roots can penetrate even in desert climes. For this reason, the date palm is most commonly found in low-lying, wet areas such as on the coast or in desert oases. Jericho, in the desert plain (Heb. *'aravah*) north of the Dead Sea, is called "the city of palm trees" in Deuteronomy 34:3 and Judges 3:13; an oasis in the

Date palm in Ashkelon on the coastal plain.

Aravah south of the Dead Sea is called, simply, Tamar (1 Kgs 9:17). Perhaps because the date palm thrives in the harshest of climates, with a strong, straight trunk, a healthy, green crown and the sweetest of fruits, it became the symbol of a righteous, upright life in the biblical world (Ps 92:12). Images of the palm tree were carved into the walls of the Jerusalem temple (1 Kgs 6:29), and struck on coins to represent Israel in the time of the New Testament. The crowds inviting Jesus to Jerusalem of course lined the way with cut palm fronds (Jn 12:13).

These seven species take their canonical form in Deuteronomy 8:8, which mirrors in broad outline the yearly calendar: grain is harvested first, in late spring and early summer, then the first summer fruit (grapes and figs) is harvested in late summer followed by pomegranates and olives in early to mid-autumn. Wheat precedes barley in the list but not in calendar order, probably to give pride of place to ancient Israel's main staple. Similarly, honey rounds out the list; if the correct reference is indeed to a paste of dates or grapes, then the last-mentioned foodstuff is the sweetest of all, finishing the yearly diet with, as it were, dessert.

A good many other plants that were helpful to human life in the biblical world can also be mentioned. These include flax (Heb. *pishtah*), which requires three times the amount of water as wheat and from which linen is spun, the almond tree (Heb. *shaqed*) which blossoms first in the spring, the apple tree (Heb. *tapuah*), the sycomore fig (Heb. *shiqmah*), the lentil (Heb. *'adashah*) and

An early spring almond blossom in the hill country of Judah.

of course chick peas, not mentioned in the Bible although domesticated samples have been found in Pre-Pottery Neolithic Jericho and across the eastern Mediterranean from the sixth millennium B.C. on. It would be hard to imagine our biblical ancestors *not* eating humus with some sort of flat bread, although the evidence for such is purely speculative.

The Bible does not provide us a comparable list of **seven species of domesticated animals** and so we might posit our own:

- **Sheep** (Heb. *seh*, plural; for other names see above). Sheep were the most important commodity of all of the peoples of the Bible, and the main measure of prosperity. Sheep provided wool for clothing (2 Kgs 3:4) and milk for protein (Deut 32:14)

A flock of sheep on Azekah in the Judean Shephelah, enjoying the springtime green.

but seldom meat unless the flock was large, for if a farmer or shepherd ate his sheep he would be consuming capital rather than allowing it to provide other commodities necessary for daily life. Even though sheep are most often associated with drier, steppe lands located in the eastern and southern parts of the southern Levant, they played an important role in the economy of villages, towns and urban areas across the entire region. Like the grape vine among plants, the sheep among animals was the proper symbol of ancient Israel, a helpless being that had to be led (Ps 23:1–6; 77:20; 78:52, 70–72; 80:1; Isa 53:6).

A goat navigating the sandstone mountains of Petra in the highlands of Edom.

- **Goat** (Heb. *'ez*; collectively, sheep and goats are both called *tzon*, "small cattle" or "flock"). A shepherd's flock is nearly always mixed, with a contingent of black (Song of Songs 1:5; 4:1; 6:5) but also spotted (Gen 30:32) goats mingling among the sheep (today, goats are also white, brown or red). Goats are an additional source of milk (Prov 27:27) and meat for the shepherd's diet. They also provide building material. The classic desert tent was—and remains—a sturdy yet movable structure woven from coarse black goat hair (e.g., Ex 26:7). The shorn hair behaves the same way for the tent that it does when still attached to the goat: it lets in air for ventilation when dry but swells to repel rainwater when wet. Goats are hardier than sheep, able to withstand drier climates and survive on more meagre fare. For this reason, the further out on the desert fringe of the steppe land the shepherd lives, the greater the proportion of goats to sheep in his flock. Eventually he and his hoofed charge reach a place where sheep can no longer survive but goats still can. Goats and sheep are both able to overgraze the land; this tendency, coupled with erratic rainfall, prompts shepherds to be mobile but also protective of the scant resources at hand (fights over water and grazing rights abound; Gen 13:6–7; 26:19–22; Ex 2:15–19). The goat's natural hardiness leads it to be individualistic and precocious, characteristics that make it a negative, rather than positive, symbol of God's people (Matt 25:32–33).
- **Large cattle** (Heb. *baqar* is the herd; *shor* is a single head). As with sheep and goats ("small cattle"), Hebrew uses several words to distinguish different kinds of "large cattle" based on gender, size and observable characteristics. Of these, the

Cattle on the basalt-strewn Golan in western Bashan.

zarzir in Prov 30:31 may refer to a strutting rooster, but that's it. Chicken bones dating to the Iron Age have been found in archaeological excavations in Jerusalem and Lachish, so the bird must have been known. Doves or pigeons (Heb. *yonah*) are much more frequently mentioned in the Bible, often wild (Song of Songs 2:14), sometimes domesticated (Isa 60:8) and everywhere present (Song of Songs 1:15; 5:2; Isa 38:14; Hos 7:11). Rock hewn dovecotes from the Hellenistic and Roman periods are frequent in the archaeological record of ancient Israel. Domesticated geese are known from paintings in ancient Egypt and from ivory carvings from Megiddo dating to the end of the Late Bronze Age (thirteenth century B.C.), making it likely that the "fattened fowl" of Solomon's table (1 Kgs 4:23) were geese. Ducks are also known in Canaanite and Egyptian art.[40] Domesticated birds were used for food (eggs and meat), fuel (dung) and, like sheep, goats and cattle, for sacrifice.

generic term *baqar* includes both cattle and oxen. Cattle of a number of breeds were common across the ancient world. They and their herdsmen are displayed in all manner of real life situations in stone-carved and/or painted Egyptian reliefs. Cattle were kept everywhere in ancient Israel as well. The Bible speaks of cattle on the coastal plain (1 7:21), in the Shephelah (2 Chron 26:10), in the hill country of Israel (Gen 18:1, 8) and in Gilead, out in marginal steppe lands (Gen 4:20; 13:2; Num 32:1) and up on the highlands of the Golan (Bashan; Ps 22;12; Amos 4:1) and Edom (Isa 34:7). The writers of the Bible paid particular attention to the size and strength of cattle, often contrasting those characteristics with the frailty of people. Because of their size, cattle consumed a relatively large quantity of local resources (water, grazing land and/or grain)—especially so the "fatted calf" (1 Kgs 4:23)—and so we might suppose that a common village farmer would own only a very small number, if more than just one. Cattle provided milk (Gen 18:8), meat (Matt 22:4) and labor, and served as draught animals (Deut 25:4; 1 Sam 6:10–12; 1 Kgs 19:19; Lk 14:19).

- **Domesticated fowl** (Heb. *'of*; although this word is generic for all types of flying creatures). Chickens, domesticated in India, have become the world's most widespread domesticated bird, but if we expect to find them throughout the biblical record we will be disappointed. Jesus compared his care for Jerusalem to that which a hen (Gk. *nossia*) has for its chicks; the cock, or rooster (Gk. *alektor*) makes a prominent appearance in the trial of Jesus before Caiaphas (Matt 26:34, 74–75); and the hapax

A donkey plowing the fields of the hill country of Ephraim.

A chicken depicted in mosaic on the floor of the south aisle of the 5th–6th century A.D. Byzantine church at Petra, Jordan. The aisle depicts personifications of Wisdom, Earth, Ocean and the Four Seasons.

- **Donkey** (Heb. *hamor*). Like sheep, goats and cattle, donkeys are everywhere in the biblical record, referenced by a variety of terms and found in every ecosystem. Their coat is red-brown (tawny; Judg 5:10) or grey, their muscles hardened and their disposition determined (for better or worse). Donkeys have sure-footed staying power that allows them to persist in any climate, terrain or situation of life; like the olive tree, they are a "fast friend of worthless soil." Donkeys are less expensive to buy and maintain than are cattle, and hence are more prevalent as a working animal (Ezra 2:66–67). They were the beast of burden of nearly everyone in the ancient world, commoner as well as king, at least in peacetime (Gen 42:26–27; Ex 4:20;

Num 22:21; Judg 10:4; 1 Sam 16:20; 2 Sam 19:26; 1 Kgs 2:40; Isa 30:6; Zech 9:9), and the chief draught animal across the southern Levant (Deut 22:10; Isa 30:24). Like sheep, the number of donkeys owned was a sure indicator of personal or family wealth (Gen 30:43; Judg 10:4; Job 1:3).

A herd of camels grazing on late winter growth in the Judean Wilderness.

- **Camel** (Heb. *gamal*). The light-brown, single-humped ship of the desert is perhaps the most exotic animal of the biblical world. The camel's broad, padded hooves, its ability to store fat in its hump and water in its stomach, and its transparent inner eyelids make it ideally suited for long-distance, sand-blown desert travel (Isa 60:6; 1 Kgs 10:2). As such, camels linked the land ports of Transjordan with the shipping lanes of the eastern desert as surely as the sea ports of Phoenicia linked Canaan with the Mediterranean. But it would be a mistake limit the camel's usefulness to these nether regions. The camel's superior size (Matt 19:24; 23:24), strength and endurance made it an important beast of burden throughout all of the ecosystems of the biblical world. While clear evidence for the domestication of the camel prior to the twelfth century B.C. is lacking in the archaeological record,[41] the frequent mention of camels in the patriarchal narratives depicts a widespread, time-honored human adaptation to the great desert expanse framing the southeastern Levant.
- **Horse** (Heb. *sus*). If the palm tree and its honey was the exceptional element of the daily diet in the biblical world, so the horse was the most extraordinary of ancient Israel's domesticated animals. The horse of course is not native to the Middle East but rather to the steppes of central Asia. Once introduced to Canaan, it found its most feared role as a draught animal linked to the chariots of the Hyksos, a Canaanite people who ruled over Egypt in the seventeenth and sixteenth centuries B.C. (the 15th dynasty). The horse became the engine of the world's most feared war machine, Pharaoh's New Kingdom army. From there it was reintroduced to prominence in the southern Levant under the royal administration of Solomon, who saw himself as the heir to Egyptian imperial dominance in the region (Song of Songs 1:9). Solomon indeed controlled the import and export of horses across the eastern seaboard of the Mediterranean (1 Kgs 10:26–29), a sure sign that the isolated ecosystem of Jerusalem could dominate the entire Levant if its resources could be harnessed as one. The horse remained more an instrument of war than a tool of transport in ancient Israel, a living resource that represented imperial might (Job 39:19–25; Isa 22:7, 31:1; Mic 1:13) rather than the home-grown efforts of tending the land.

The usefulness of plants and animals to the people of the biblical world might best be measured by their value in supplying food. Commodity lists from the Bible and other ancient texts, as well as information that can be deduced from archaeology and physical geography, indicate that the ancient Israelites enjoyed a diet that was quite healthy, though relatively limited in variety. The various ecosystems of the southern Levant produced an acceptable mixture of meat and animal products, fruits, vegetables and grains. The ideal was to have something from each of the local food groups at least once in a while. Folks living in the seams between ecosystems had an advantage, as did people in port cities that relied on trade. Jesse of Bethlehem, for instance, sent products of the field (parched grain—probably wheat—and loaves of bread) to David as his son squared off against the Philistines, and products of the flock (cuts of cheese) to David's commander (1 Sam 17:17–18). This menu might be expected from someone living in a town on the seam between the land of the farmer and the land of the shepherd, although in practice most thriving villages were able to maintain a mixed economy just about anywhere in the land. As an aside, we note that in sending these provisions, Jesse favored the commander over his own son—the former received protein-rich cheese, a clever way of ensuring that one's flesh and blood would receive favor in turn when it really counted. Years later, David and his wilderness-weary men received a much larger meal from his Transjordanian supporters as he fled his son, Absalom:

> *. . . wheat, barley, flour, parched grain, beans, lentils, parched seeds, honey, curds, sheep and cheese of the herd.*
>
> 2 Samuel 17:28–29

Quite a feast, which is a blend of foods representing the ecosystems of a Judean-Gilead connection that spanned the Rift Valley. But it was David's primary son and heir, Solomon, who feasted the best:

> *Solomon's provision for one day was thirty kor [i.e., 185 bushels/6.5 kiloliters] of fine flour, sixty kor of meal, ten fat oxen, twenty pasture-fed oxen, a hundred sheep besides deer, gazelles, roebucks and fattened fowl.*
>
> 1 Kings 4:22–23

Clearly this daily feast was not meant for Solomon alone but also for his retainers, dependents and government officials. More importantly, Solomon's diet came from ecosystems far afield of the Judean hill country. Indeed, his hunting grounds covered the entire Levant, "everything west of the [Euphrates] River, from Tiphsah as far as Gaza" (1 Kgs 4:24), a super market fit for a king (cp. 1

The war horse and chariot of Pharaoh Ramses II depicted in pitched battle on a wall in the Ramesseum temple, on the West Bank of the Nile in Luxor (ancient Thebes), Egypt.

Thistles are pokey when green, even more so when dried. They appear in throughout the land in many varieties; this one is a Cotton Thistle standing sentinel in Upper Galilee.

I will break down its wall and it will become trampled ground....

Isaiah 5:5

*Why have You broken down its hedges
     so that all who pass that way will pick its fruit?
A boar from the forest eats it away
     and whatever moves in the field feeds on it.*

Psalm 80:12–13

*I will lay it waste; it will not be pruned or hoed,
     but briars and thorns will come up....*

Isaiah 5:6

Kgs 10:26–29). The writer of 1 Kings is quick to follow up with the local diet of Solomon's contented subjects: "*every man under his vine and fig tree*" (1 Kgs 4:25), an indication that the most essential ecosystem of ancient Judah was the hard limestone hill country.

The Bible preserves other lists of plants and animals as menus.[42] Bread cakes of fine flower, a tender and choice calf, curds and milk served as Abraham's offered fare to desert travelers who came upon his tent (Gen 18:6–8). Abigail, wife of a certain Nabal who grazed three thousand sheep and one thousand goats in the steppe land between Carmel and Maon southeast of Hebron, offered David and his men a meal fit for a *sheikh*: loaves of bread, wine, sheep, roasted grain, raisin clusters, and fig cakes (1 Sam 25:18). It was a meal that included plenty of staples, the extravagance of meat, and dessert. And meat was extravagant. The Passover Meal, in which a lamb is slaughtered for food (Ex 12:5), marks a significant moment of time in a family's local economy, as does any occasion to celebrate by "*killing the fatted calf*" (Gen 18:7–8; Lk 15:23). In contrast, Ezekiel baked bread with a recipe that represented siege food: wheat, barley, beans, lentils, millet and spelt, likely the bits and pieces of whatever was left in his cupboard (Ezek 4:9). For their part, the comrades of Elisha resorted to the time-honored practice of hunting and gathering during famine, harvesting "*a wild vine*" (Heb. *gefen sadeh*, lit. "vine of the field") and "*wild gourds*" (Heb. *paqqu'ot sadeh*, perhaps cucumbers) which turned out to be mildly poisonous (2 Kgs 4:38–41). For all of this, we can probably assume that the list of insects declared by Leviticus 11:21–23 as clean to eat betrays a reality that for most of the people most of the time, the main food group was composed of grubs, little lizards, bugs and whatever else happened to move slower than the hunter. When John the Baptist, raised like his father to be a priest in Jerusalem, was reduced to eating locust in the Judean Wilderness, at least he could keep kosher—and locust are high in protein and fat with plenty of riboflavin and Vitamin B[2].

At the other end of the usefulness spectrum are plants and animals that harm people, threaten domesticated livestock or damage crops. These include a long list of weeds, thorns and thistles that seem to grow everywhere. "*Cursed is the ground because of you,*" after Adam's first sin God announced that "*both thorns and thistles it shall grow for you*" (Gen 3:17–19), and the land does seem to have a disproportionately large number of kinds of thistles for its size. The ground of the southern Levant is rocky and hard enough as it is—is a natural undergrowth of thorny shrubs and thistles really all that necessary? The land does seem to revert to an uncultivated state rather quickly without constant care:

*So now let Me tell you what I am going to do to My vineyard:
     I will remove its hedge and it will be consumed;*

The serpent (Heb. *nahash*) is the first animal mentioned by name in the Bible (Gen 3:1), and it leads a long list of critters harmful or bothersome to human activity. These include the lion (Heb. *'ari*, etc.), bear (Heb. *dov*), hyena (Heb. *tzebo'im*, pl.), wild boar (Heb. *hazir*), scorpion (Heb. *'aqrab*, including the yellow-white "Death Stalker"), locust of many kinds (Joel 1:4), little foxes (Heb. *shu'alim*) that ruin the vineyards (Song of Songs 2:15), and birds of prey such as the eagle (Heb. *nesher*), vulture (Heb. *nesher* or *peres*) and raven (Heb. *'oreb*; 1 Kgs 17:6. Would you eat carrion from the mouth of a raven?). Flies (Heb. *zebub*) represented for the biblical writer what we know to be a host of flying insects that are bothersome at best (Ex 8:16–29). The ancients did not recognize the beneficial role that plants and animals such as these played in the ecosystems of the southern Levant; rather, such creatures were grouped together with the destructive forces of nature to represent by metaphor what they were in the practical terms of everyday life:

The yellow-green "death stalker" scorpion, deadly to humans and still common in the highlands of Edom.

The griffon vulture in morning flight.

The fox, characteristically curious, here at Gamla on the Golan Heights.

Fire and hail and famine and pestilence,
*   all these have been created for vengeance;*
the teeth of wild beasts, and scorpions and vipers,
*   and the sword that punishes the ungodly with destruction . . .*

Sirach 39:29–30

A large host of plant and animal life that is neither normally domesticated nor necessarily seen as harmful for human life fills the land, sky or sea, or lurks out on the borders of settled activity. The waters "teem with swarms of living creatures," the "open expanse of heaven" is crossed with birds in flight, and animals, together with people, "fill the earth" below (Gen 1:20–21, 28). Sometimes these plants and animals play a role in the biblical story; more often they are "just there." Local inhabitants knew the properties of each growing plant: which leaf or root or shoot could cure which ailment, which greenery made the best broth or tea; which wood was best suited for kindling or for fashioning agricultural implements, and so on. Examples are endless; mention of just a few will suffice. The hard wood of the desert acacia (Heb. *shittim*) makes excellent lumber (Ex 25:10, 23), while that of the broom tree (Heb. *rotem*) is used for charcoal (Ps 120:4). The coriander (Heb. *gad*) is mentioned in the Bible only to try to explain what manna was by comparison (Ex 16:31); its constituent parts are nevertheless useful as a condiment for cooking and for medicine. The strong, crooked branches of the Tabor oak (Heb. *allon*) and terebinth (Heb. *elah*) serve as useful lumber from which to form agricultural implements such as plows and yokes. In the springtime wildflowers abound—they, in particular, attract bees which produce the other kind of honey (Judg. 14:8). The partridge (Heb. *qore'*, lit. "the caller") and the quail (Heb. *selau*) are game birds, adding protein to a diet that otherwise was reticent to include the meat of domesticated animals. The partridge makes its home in the hill country (1 Sam 26:20; Jer 17:11) but the quail migrates to the southern Levant in the spring, following the wind (Ex 16:13). Game animals include the deer (Heb. *'ayyal*), fallow deer (Heb. *yahmur*), gazelle (Heb. *tzvi*) and ibex (*ya'el*), all sure-footed, quick and beautiful to behold in the wild (Gen 49:21; 1 Kgs 4:23; Ps 42:1; 104:18; Song of Songs 2:7; Isa 13:14).

A separate category, somewhat unique to ancient Israel, delineates clean from unclean animals, namely, those which may or may not be consumed as food (Lev 11:1–47; Deut 14:3–20). There is not a similar delineation of clean and unclean plants. In any case, a variety of suggestions have been made as to what the point of these laws was for ancient Israel[43] (the reason for keeping kosher among observant Jews today is a related, though not identical, subject). It can be noted that some of the animals considered to be clean (and hence edible) were from the domestic stock (the ox, sheep and goat) while others were hunted (the deer, fallow deer, gazelle and ibex, among others). The existence of these dietary regulations, whatever their reason for being, is evidence enough that the Israelites knew the details of their living environment and were adept at both observing and classifying large parts of it. This brings us back to Solomon, with whom this chapter began, an astute observer of life. Solomon spoke:

of trees, from the cedar that is in Lebanon even to the hyssop that grows on the wall; he spoke also of animals and birds and creeping things and fish.

1 Kings 4:32

The clear indication is that the ancient Israelites not only knew their living environment, but, for all of its rocky, thorny and parched shortcomings, they were

glad that they shared space with its creatures. Were birds flying around inside the Temple and nesting beside its altar (Ps 84:3)? Good! God made them, too, and cares for them whether they fly or fall (Matt 6:26; 10:29). But many animals remained mysterious, their ways either unobserved or beyond human comprehension:

Do you know the time the mountain goats give birth?
*   Do you observe the calving of the deer? . . .*
Who freed the wild donkey
*   and who loosed the bonds of the swift donkey,*
*   to whom I have the wilderness for a home*
*   and the salt land for his dwelling place?...*
Will the wild ox consent to serve you,
*   or will he spend the night at your manger?...*
Is it by your understanding that the hawk soars,
*   stretching his wings toward the south?*
Is it at your command that the eagle mounts up
*   and makes his nest on high?...*

Job 39:1, 5–6, 9, 26–27

These animals, neither domesticated nor feared, lived in Job's world and he in theirs. Their world was a place teeming with life, its human occupants possessing a healthy respect for what could neither be known nor controlled (Job 42:1–6).

A final category of plants and animals are those which are valuable for long distance trade, whether exported from the southern Levant or imported in. From these we learn more about economic interdependence and trade patterns than we do about the sustainability of local ecosystems *per se*. Most goods traded beyond the borders of the southern Levant were luxuries, things not really necessary for life but rather commodities that indicated wealth, prestige, or power—or that spiced up living conditions that were otherwise rather mundane. The young Joseph was sold by his brothers to a caravan of Ishmaelites headed to Egypt carrying aromatic gum

SOLOMON'S TRADE MONOPOLY

The traders and merchants... and all the kings of Arabia and the governors of the land brought gold and silver to Solomon. (2 Chron 9:14)

From Ophir: Monkeys, parrots, gold, ivory, sandalwood, precious stones

From Sheba: Perfumes, gold, precious stones, spices

KINGS OF ARABIA

© Carta Jerusalem

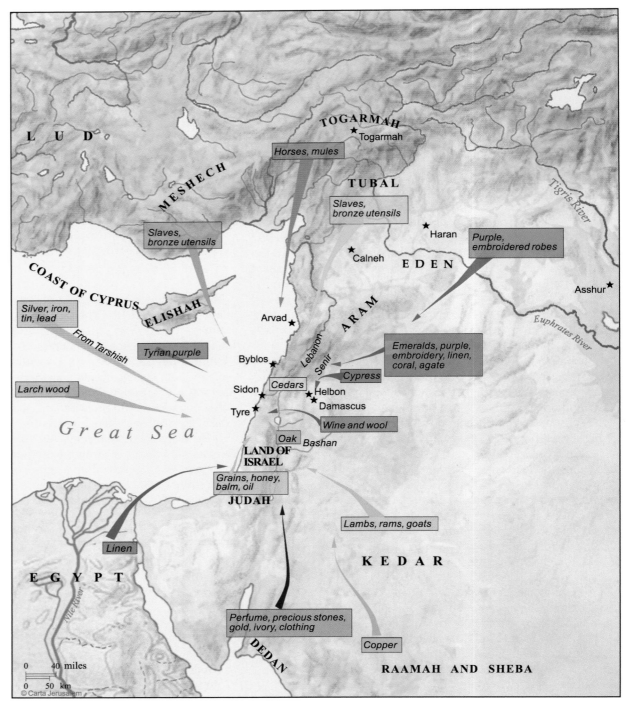

Map labels:
- L U D
- MESHECH
- TOGARMAH ★ Togarmah
- TUBAL
- Slaves, bronze utensils
- Horses, mules
- ★ Haran
- ★ Calneh
- E D E N
- ★ Asshur
- Purple, embroidered robes
- Tigris River
- COAST OF CYPRUS
- ELISHAH
- ★ Arvad
- ARAM
- Euphrates River
- Silver, iron, tin, lead
- From Tarshish
- Tyrian purple
- Byblos ★
- Lebanon
- Senir
- Emeralds, purple, embroidery, linen, coral, agate
- Larch wood
- Cedars
- Sidon ★
- Helbon ★
- Cypress
- Tyre ★
- ★ Damascus
- Great Sea
- Wine and wool
- Oak Bashan
- LAND OF ISRAEL
- Grains, honey, balm, oil
- JUDAH
- Lambs, rams, goats
- K E D A R
- Linen
- E G Y P T
- Nile River
- Perfume, precious stones, gold, ivory, clothing
- DEDAN
- Copper
- RAAMAH AND SHEBA
- 0   40 miles
- 0   50 km
- © Carta Jerusalem

(Heb. *nak'ot*), balm (Heb. *tzori*) and myrrh (Heb. *lot*; the more common Hebrew word for myrrh is *mor*) (Gen 37:25). These are the by-products of plants used in medicines, for perfume, and for embalming (Jn 19:39), all commodities very marketable in Egypt. The specific identity of each is uncertain, due in part to their non-native origin. This particular caravan originated in southern Arabia and picked up additional products on the way: balm in Gilead (Jer 8:22) and the newly-minted slave Joseph in Dothan.

A list of six exotic species available in the southern Levant for export is given in Genesis 43:11: balm, honey, aromatic gum, myrrh, pistachio nuts and almonds. Jacob described these as "some of the best products of the land" even though he certainly had acquired aromatic gum and myrrh by trade himself. Much later in the biblical narrative, the prophet Ezekiel went to great length to describe the role of Tyre in world trade of the sixth century B.C. Ezekiel provides a lengthy list of pricey goods that reached the markets of Tyre from all of the corners of the ancient world, including gold, spices, saddle blankets, embroidered cloth, carpets of many colors

with tightly wound cords, bronze vessels, ivory, ebony, tin and lead (Ezek 27:12–24). Judah and Israel's contribution to the system was wheat, honey, oil and balm, things rather mundane by comparison but vital for traders who were either too busy, too landless or too mobile to grow sufficient food of their own. Ezekiel also takes time to describe the network that supplied materials to build and maintain the ships that carried the trade goods (Ezek 27:4–9): fir from Senir (Mt. Hermon) for the planks, cedar from Lebanon for the mast, oaks from Bashan for the oars, linen from Egypt for the sail, and so on. Any modern technician in materials handling would be proud. But perhaps the single greatest trader in the Bible was King Solomon, whose ability to control the world's economy supplanted that of the pharaohs of Egypt. Solomon, we read, imported to Jerusalem cedar and cypress from Lebanon (1 Kgs 5:6, 8), gold, almug trees and precious stones from Ophir (1 Kgs 10:11), and silver, ivory, apes, peacocks, garments, weapons, spices, horses and mules in large seagoing vessels of the Tarshish type that plied the waters of the Mediterranean and Red Seas (1 Kgs 10:22, 25).

E. "FOR HE LOVED THE SOIL" — 2 CHRONICLES 26:10

Nearly eighty years ago, in his presidential address to the Association of American Geographers, Carl Ortwin Sauer spoke of the need to fuse physical geography with human geography. In doing so, he pled for the relevance of something called historical geography, the study of historical processes within culture areas, regions that are defined by their modes of living as well as their physical characteristics.

> A culture area, as a community with a way of living, is…a growth on a particular "soil" or home, an historical and geographical expression. Its mode of living, economy, or *Wirtschaft* is its way of maximizing the satisfactions it seeks and of minimizing the efforts it expends. That is perhaps what adaptation to environment means. In terms of its knowledge at the time, the group is making proper or full use of its site…. Such study of cultural areas is historical geography.[44]

Sauer called for students of historical geography to focus their efforts on cultural ecology, the study of the processes by which a society adapts culturally, rather than simply biologically, to the environment which it calls home. In plain terms, he advocated for an emphasis on cultural, rather than biological, evolution. According to Sauer, the basic criterion of cultural ecology is how people learn to make a living off their land, with the most relevant pool of data that which is grounded in what the land itself has to offer, rather than what is brought in via conquest or trade.

The cultural ecologist might ask a variety of questions. For instance, what are the interrelationships between productive technologies (i.e., technologies that aid a person's ability to live in their chosen environment) and the environment itself? To what extent do these technologies blend in with the environment, or, conversely, seek to alter it? What social structures arise from the demands of the environment in which a particular people group lives? How, in the instance of the biblical world, does the ecology of desert steppe land affect human social structures and values, and how might those differ from ones that arise in highland villages or in urban centers on the plain? Under what conditions is cooperation between culture areas fostered and competition tempered, and vice versa? What geographical features tend to connect a cultural area with its neighbor? What features serve to isolate one area from the next? And what effect does the physical world in which people live shape their understanding of what might lie beyond, of the reason and essence of their existence? The bases of human cultural adaptation to any given ecosystem may be manipulative and economic, but in the world of the Bible there was also a spiritual side. (There still is.) To speak biblically, how does the God Who Lies Beyond interact in tangible, earthy and humanly productive ways with the living beings that he created? And how do those beings live in harmony with the land that he made for their home?

These are all big questions. Any attempt at addressing them requires an exhaustive familiarity with specific landscapes of the past and the human processes which unfolded on them. Sauer continues:

> The reconstruction of critical cultural landscapes of the past [by the historical geographer] requires (a) knowledge of the functioning of the given culture as a whole, (b) a control of all the contemporary evidences…and (c) the most intimate familiarity with the terrain which the given culture occupied….
>
> One might say that [the historical geographer] needs **the ability to see the land with the eyes of its former occupants** [my emphasis], from the standpoint of their needs and capacities. This is about the most difficult task in all human geography: to evaluate site and situation, not from the standpoint of an educated American of today [for instance], but to place oneself in the position of a member of the cultural group at the time being studied.[45]

Sauer's plea that we attempt to see a landscape through the eyes of its former inhabitants (in our case, its biblical ones) is on target, as is his assessment that the task of doing so is both challenging and problematic. We search for an insider's view of the past. The goal is impossible, really, though we can gain a reasonable approximation of it by combining information drawn from texts written by the group being studied with a diligent inquiry of their geographical, archaeological, and cultural environments.

The Bible recognizes the wide variety of cultural areas, or ecosystems, that made up the lands of ancient Israel and its neighbors, and gives witness to the complex interrelationships between them. Its pages are also infused with the idea that human life cannot be lived *except in* connection with the God-infused natural world that envelopes its beings. Much of the textual data that we might seek in order to gain an understanding of the ecological awareness of ancient Israel is not obvious precisely because it was so much a part of everyday life that it did not need to be mentioned by the biblical authors. What we need is to sharpen our eyes to see data that lurks between the lines. A few examples, each drawn from a different slice through the available data, can be given.

First, an example of shepherding. Many of the shepherds that we meet on the pages of the Bible (e.g., David, Nabal and the shepherds who visited the infant Jesus) were attached to a particular village and grazed their sheep on commonly held village lands, usually within the close proximity of home. If environmental conditions necessitated, the village shepherd might drive his flocks further afield, such as deep into the Judean Wilderness, for days or even weeks at a time. Even so, the shepherd's economic and social unit remained the members of his extended family or the clan that comprised his home village. Other shepherds (e.g., the Patriarchs and Moses, in his second career) better fit the category of semi-nomads, persons at home in the arid steppe lands that lie between permanent villages and the open desert and move their tent encampments with the seasons. While both types of shepherds were intimately familiar with the needs and behaviors of their flocks (Prov 27:23), it was the semi-nomadic shepherds who had a greater need to develop symbiotic, mutually-advantageous relationships with specific villages or urban centers that lay alongside their extended grazing zone.[46] Here a shepherd forged relationships with people groups that were not part of his extended family, clan or tribe, a process that fostered the development of survival skills in a world that was otherwise based on established bloodline ties. These skills included protocols of hospitality that built levels of trust that were necessary

Sheep in the Buqe'a valley in the eastern Judean Wilderness, a region where flocks attached to a village meet those of semi-nomadic Bedouin.

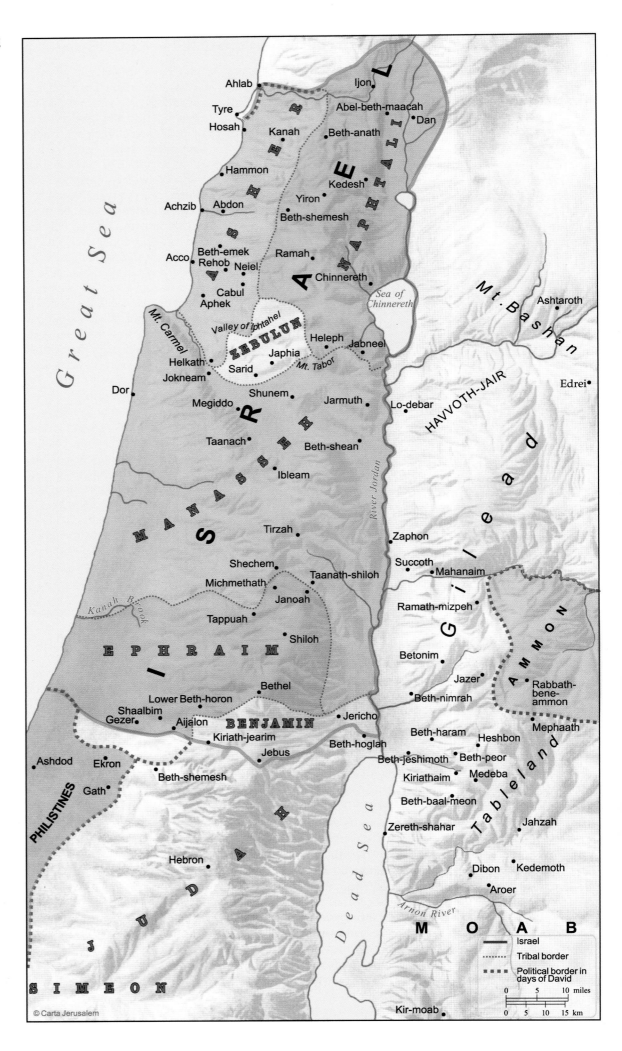

© Carta Jerusalem

——	Israel
······	Tribal border
▪▪▪▪	Political border in days of David

0   5   10 miles

0   5   10   15 km

for mutual economic and social cooperation, and hence survival. Abraham's experiences in Shechem, Gerar and Hebron, all large Canaanite urban centers in his day, need to be seen in this light (Gen 12:6–7; 20:1–18; 23:1–20). His tent encampment in Beer-sheba, on the other hand, a place with only a tamarisk tree and a well (Gen 21:27–34; cf. 26:1–33), lay a bit beyond the twelve-inch rainfall line and hence was a place close enough to the Canaanite cities to conduct trade but not so close so as to threaten their economic well-being. The urban centers that lined these steppe lands, cities such as Jerusalem, Hebron and Gerar, became market towns, where the products of the shepherd were exchanged for the products of the farmer, strengthening mutual economic and social ties in the process. For centuries, the northeastern corner of Jerusalem had a Sheep Gate (Neh 3:1; Jn 5:2), with the sheep market just outside (the market persisted there until the 1980's), and it was in such locations that the processes of cooperation and competition were most keenly felt.

Ancient Israel's founding fathers were shepherds of the semi-nomadic kind, and the values that they espoused—hospitality, loyalty within blood ties, provision and protection for those "in the tent," and the necessity of fighting for the right to use the scant resources at hand—became part of the core fiber of their descendants who settled the land of ancient Israel. Israel's founding king was a shepherd of the village kind, and David, like Abraham and Moses, devoted every fiber of his being to keeping his sheep alive (Jn 10:11). As docile, helpless animals, sheep don't need much—except everything that is necessary for life, and for which they are wholly dependent on their shepherds to provide. So the Psalmist, speaking of Israel's founding experiences, likened his people to a flock and their leader to a shepherd:

> [God] led forth his own people like sheep
>   and guided them in the wilderness like a flock;
> He led them is safety so that they did not fear....
> [Then] He also chose David His servant
>   and took him from the sheepfolds,
> from the care of the ewes with suckling lambs
>   he brought him to shepherd Jacob His people
>   and Israel His inheritance.
> So [David] shepherded them according to the integrity of his heart,
>   and guided them with his skillful hands.
>   Psalm 78:52–53, 70–72; cf. Micah 7:14

By metaphor, the requisite skills needed to keep sheep alive were possessed by Jesus, the Good Shepherd, and his lead disciple, Peter: "Tend my sheep" (Jn 10:11; 21:15–17). Shepherds normally get short shrift in our understanding of their role in the Gospel narrative (it is often held that the shepherds who visited the baby Jesus represented the dirty underclass of society), but a fair reading of the Old Testament shows that shepherds embody the deepest imagery of devotion and care possible. The Psalmist rightly compared God himself to a shepherd. This is the ontological key to our most substantive understanding of who God is: Creator, but also Sustainer, one who cares foremost about the life and well-being of his helpless human creatures.

A second example can be drawn from the tribal boundary descriptions and city lists that are recorded in Joshua 13–19. Although these documents certainly arose from specific political or administrative contexts in ancient Israel,[47] they also demonstrate that each tribe maintained an on-going ecological relationship with the particular territory that was its home. In most instances there is a general correspondence of the tribal boundaries to a geographically homogenous region: Asher with the seaward Acco Plain; Zebulun with the hard limestone ridges and fertile valleys of Western Lower Galilee; Issachar with the wind-swept basalt slopes of Eastern Lower Galilee; Napthali with the rugged limestone hills of Upper Galilee

The land of Naphtali northwest of the Sea of Galilee, where the terrain favors animals that have room to be wild and free.

and their sharp drop into the Rift Valley; Dan (in its second, more permanent location) at the powerful springs of Mount Hermon; Gad with the Gilead highlands and Reuben with the flat Madaba Plateau (the Mishor) east of the Rift, both places suitable for grazing (Num 32:1–5); Simeon with the arid Negev Basin surrounding Beer-sheba; and the Joseph tribes (Ephraim and Manasseh) with the rolling limestone hill country south of the Jezreel Valley. By contrast, only the tribal inheritances of Judah and Benjamin were more diverse geographically. While all of the tribes shared an identity of being "Israelite," as well as general characteristics that were common to being a part of the ancient Near East, specifics of lifestyle and livelihood varied with the resources and natural routes available in each of their homelands.

This ecological reality is also apparent in a different genre of tribal inheritance texts, namely, the blessings given by Jacob to his twelve sons (Genesis 49) and by Moses to the same twelve which, by his day, had become tribes (Deuteronomy 33). Taken as a whole, these blessings relate not so much to some abstract future for each eponymous ancestor and its tribal descendants but rather to the real-life conditions of their tribal homelands. As such, the blessings communicate something about the essence of each tribe's relationship to its own land, a reality that transcends individual political configurations or specific moments in time. In short, they are statements of ecology and adaptation first, and political prognoses only secondarily. Space precludes a full analysis; a few representative instances of the more obvious examples will have to suffice. Joseph's blessings abound in spring and terrace imagery, "the blessings that lie beneath" and fruitful boughs "that run over a wall" (Gen 49:22–26; Deut 33:13–17). These are characteristics of the hard limestone hill country that was his tribal home. Judah's land was similar in composition; his blessing also included lush summer fruit (Gen 49:11–12). Naphtali is "a doe (Heb. 'ayyalah) let loose" to gambol among the hills, a wild and free image consistent with an inheritance up on Israel's unbounded northern frontier (Gen 49:21). Issachar's dry, eastern-facing, boulder-strewn hills preclude easy settlement; his was a land of sheepfolds and tents, where brute strength ensured survival (Gen 49:14–15; Deut 33:18). Dan was "a lion's whelp (Heb. gur 'aryeh) leaping from [the direction of] Bashan"—a precise description of both habitat and inhabitant (Deut 33:22). The opportunities for "rich food" and "royal dainties" are

A goat hair tent in Wadi Rum, south Jordan, pitched with ageless technology.

no better apparent than out on Asher's Acco Plain, the location of ancient Israel's only natural seaport and its best source of luxury goods (Gen 49:20). Sometimes the blessings speak not so much about the obvious aspects of a tribal land's ecology as its historical-geographical role. Reuben, for instance, inherited the Mishor east of the Dead Sea, a land that, due to its open position, was continually overrun by invaders from all sides. The land itself reflects (or maybe caused?) Reuben's inability to sustain its tribal identity over time. Jacob decried Reuben's lack of preeminence (he was, after all, the firstborn) and Moses plead that Reuben not die out (Gen 49:3–4; Deut 33:6), statements that are "Oh. Of course." once we see the edgy ecosystem that Reuben called home.

A third example of the Bible's awareness of differing ecosystems and their cultural interactions within the land of ancient Israel has to do with the geographical relationship between Israel's earliest settlement activities and the Canaanite cities (or city-states). By the time that Israel entered the land of Canaan to settle down (the end of the Late Bronze Age and beginning of Iron Age I), the Canaanite cities were old, well-established entities, each largely in charge of their own territories' natural resources. Many were under some level of Egyptian imperial control, but even as Egyptian agents they actively utilized the resources under their care, including long-established networks of commerce and trade. The Canaanites were urban people, living, as it were, "on the grid." In contrast, the Israelites, who had learned to live "off the grid" during their forty years of wilderness wandering in the wastelands of the Sinai, continued to do so even after they had penetrated Canaan. A careful reading of the city lists and boundary descriptions of ancient Israel shows that the Israelite tribes essentially entered into, then filled up, land that lay *between* the Canaanite cities. While each Canaanite city was the center of a functioning economic unit that included a circle of dependent villages and their shared, landed resources, for Israel these cities were border points on the frontiers of individual tribes (e.g., Josh 18:12, 13, 16; 19:10, etc.). After the Canaanite cities fell—a process that was largely coextensive with the early periods of Israel's penetration of the land—their ruins were rebuilt by Israel, though not to the same level of urbanization. In spite of a gradual move toward their own forms of urbanization, a process which gained real strength only in the eighth century B.C., Israel maintained its old-time, tent-dwelling tribal ideal as somehow being more authentic of its own identity. Hence Isaiah, a resident of Jerusalem when the city was at the peak of its urban glory, who spoke of restoring the city after its impending desolation as if it were a Bedouin tent:

> Enlarge the place of our tent;
>> Stretch out the curtains of your dwellings, do not spare [any
>> effort or material];
> Lengthen your cords
>> and strengthen your pegs.

Isaiah 54:2

And why not? Isaiah had used the same imagery to describe the creation of the cosmos, God's tent of provision and protection in which his people would dwell (Isa 40:22; 42:5; 44:24; 45:12). The prophet Zephaniah, who was not only a resident of Jerusalem in the heady days of Josiah but a direct descendant of Hezekiah and hence party to the comforts of urban life, spoke similarly. Zephaniah looked forward to the day when the prosperous and interconnected coastal cities, which in his vision had become grid-locked, would be replaced by Israel's shepherding ideal:

> So the seacoast will be pastures,
>> with caves for shepherds and folds for flocks.
> And the coast will be for the remnant of the house of Judah;
>> they will pasture on it.
> In the houses of Ashkelon they will lie down at evening;
>> for the LORD their God will care for them and restore their
>> fortune.

Zephaniah 2:6–7

The biblical authors continually shifted between recognizing the benefits of the land's two major ecosystems, one of the shepherd, the other the successful village farmer which, given the right circumstances and passage of time, developed into urban centers. Fully cognizant of both, the self-understanding of the people of the Book—whether they be its authors or characters on its pages—can be seen through the reality of the varied landscapes of ancient Israel which, collectively, they called home. While we take their awareness of the created, natural world for granted, we must not minimize its effects on their being. We might think it apparent that people who spent most of their years away from urban centers, folk such as Abraham, Moses, David and Jesus, were closely connected to the throb of the land, and be right in doing so. But so was the Jerusalemite Isaiah, whose book is so jammed with intimate knowledge of the world of nature that it is reasonable to assume that he, like many who were drawn to the city, maintained a real tie to his ancestral lands. And of course the royal houses of both Israel and Judah also had landed prerogatives. We may focus on their misuse, such as when Ahab seized the land of Naboth to convert a productive vineyard into a mere (though royal) vegetable patch, disinheriting its rightful owner and lowering the value of his land in the process (1 Kgs 21:2). But the opposite was certainly also true. Judah's good king Uzziah, whose reign in the mid-eighth century B.C. coincided with a time of rising prosperity and burgeoning cities, built

> [watch]towers in the wilderness and hewed many cisterns, for he had much livestock, both in the lowland and in the plain. He also had plowmen and vinedressers in the hill country and the fertile fields, for he loved the soil [Heb. 'adamah hayah, "the ground of life"].

2 Chronicles 26:10

This was the royal equivalent of the sobriquet "every man lived under his own vine and fig tree" (1 Kgs 4:25), and assumes a healthy cooperation between people and land at all levels of society, including its inhabitants who were separated from their lands on a daily basis.

* * * * *

Ancient Israel's world-awareness held that creation was both good and very good (Gen 1:10, 12, 18, 21, 25, 31), that is to say, perfectly suited for harmonious existence among all living things. At the same time, the Genesis creation account includes the command that people "fill," "subdue" and "rule over" the rest of creation (Gen

A modern example of ecological awareness run amuck. This is the water of the Kidron Valley deep in the Judean Wilderness, flowing with raw sewage, plastic and broken pieces of manmade waste.

1:28). While the practical import of these verbs remains the subject of lively debate, they do seem to embrace the idea that people, made in the image of God, are creative and therefore have the capacity (and perhaps even the right) to utilize the created order for their own good. But there can be a very fine line between caretaking (Gen 2:15) and exploiting, between developing the natural world and altering it to its own harm, and between consequences that are unintended and those that intentionally destroy land, water or air. A study of the cultural ecology of the Bible reveals the interminable tug between responsibility and dominance, in the process preserving ample witness of human intervention at its very best, and very worst.

On the plus side, the Bible speaks out, for instance, in favor of the humane treatment of animals. A donkey or ox that has fallen or strayed or suffers under a heavy load should be helped to its feet, led home or released from its burden (Ex 23:4–5; Deut 22:4; Lk 14:5). Like people who earn their wages, an ox should not be muzzled but allowed to eat when it is threshing grain (Deut 25:4; 1 Cor 9:9; 1 Tim 5:18). Domesticated work animals need regular rest, a Sabbath, just as people do (Ex 23;11; Deut 5:14; Lk 13:15). That an ox knows its owner, a donkey its master's crib, and sheep their shepherd's voice (Isa 1:3; Jn 10:4) does not imply that these are animals are dumb and know no better, but that they respond to care. In a test of stubborn wills, Balaam was upbraided for striking his donkey, an animal that had served him faithfully for years (Num 22:22–30). Even one lost sheep out of one hundred is

worth great effort to find (Lk 15:3–6). A mother bird with eggs or young should not be caught by a passer-by but rather left to live and propagate another day, though the eggs and its young may be used as food (Deut 22:6–7). And, at the risk of contradicting millennia of halachic interpretative tradition that forms the basis of kosher laws, the Israelites were instructed no less than three times (Ex 23:19; 34:26; Deut 14:21) not to take, kill and hence boil a young goat that was still *on* (not "in;" the Hebrew preposition *b-* can mean either) its mother's milk, that is, young enough so as not to have yet been weaned.[48] That many of these examples are found in the Pentateuch's legal texts suggests that the misuse or abuse of animals (cf. Ezek 34:1–6) was more frequent in the ancient world than not. The underlying theme is one of compassion and care for animals, whether they belong to the individual so instructed, someone else, or live in the wild. But the Psalmist offers a more comprehensive view of ownership—and hence the proper justification for care—stating that every living being, whether domesticated or wild, in fact belongs to God:

> For every beast of the forest is Mine,
>   the cattle on a thousand hills.
> I know every bird of the mountains,
>   and everything that moves in the field is Mine.

Psalm 50:10–11

They all wait for You to give them their food in due season.

41

Two sheep, tied for slaughter, innocent to the details of their impending fate.

You give to them; they gather it up;
   You open Your hand, and they are satisfied with good.

                                   Psalm 104:27–28

Of course, the Psalmist punctuated his declaration with the word "good," the term that defines creation.

On several occasions the author has witnessed the slaughter of sheep or goat by a Bedouin for his family's evening meal. The moment of death is in the quick, clean cut of the animal's jugular. The adage "the life of the flesh is in the blood" (Lev 17:11) is never more apparent than in this ageless act, in which the blood of one living being is shed to provide sustenance and life for another. In one particular instance the Bedouin, a young man named Fahad al-Hawati, carefully gave his animal, which was looking rather sheepish, a long drink of water from a dish just moments before the slaughter, holding the vessel in one hand and caressing his sheep with the other. "Why?" I asked. "It will be dead within minutes. Does the water somehow help the butchering process?" "No," came the quiet reply. "We want our animals to be calm and feel that they are loved." A shepherd knows his sheep; a lamb led to the slaughter is silent, trustingly so (cf. Isa 53:7).

On the negative side, the Bible includes many instances of harm done to the land of ancient Israel, sometimes unintentionally but often with clear intent. A frequent example is overgrazing, which is more common when the land is grazed by goats, nonselective eaters, than sheep.[49] We read in Genesis that "the land could not sustain" the combined flocks of Abraham and Lot and so their herdsmen separated one from the other (Gen 13:6–12). Abraham remained in the steppe land between Bethel and Ai, the last arable tracts east of the watershed before the drop of the Judean wilderness into the Rift; Lot moved into the more fertile areas of the Jordan Valley and ended up forging symbiotic relationships, for better or worse, with the city of Sodom. Similar instances have been as frequent as they are typical among the shepherding clans of the southern Levant for millennia. The Mosaic law counseled against overgrazing, aware that its consequences naturally spread from one plot of ground to the next, then to the next (Ex 22:5). The age-old pattern of moving one's flocks with the seasons mitigated against the long-term effects of overgrazing.

More dramatic were invasions of herding tribes off of the eastern steppes and into the fields of the farmer, usually prompted by inadequate rainfall that could not sustain their customary grazing lands. The Midianites, Amalekites and "Sons of the East" routinely devastated the fields of Israel in the days of the Judges, "like locusts for number" (Judg 6:3–5), prompting Gideon's successful range war

in response. But the ravages of war could be even more horrendous. The Bible speaks of a conqueror not content just to destroy a city but also sow its ruins with salt (Judg 9:45; cf. Deut 29:23) or cover its raped fields with stones (2 Kgs 3:25). While these may be idioms, they represent the reality of wartime devastation in which structures that take generations to build are destroyed in an instant. The book of Deuteronomy recognizes the brutality of war and so gives instructions for fighting fairly (Deut 20:1–20). Included is the instruction that fruit trees should not be cut down to build siege works, with the practical reason given that they provide food. But the text adds an emotional appeal: "Is the tree of the field a man, that it should be besieged by you?" (Deut 20:19).

When we bring productive technology into the equation, the results can be remarkable. The hard limestone hill country of Judah, Ephraim, Manasseh and Gilead, the heartland of the biblical story, is by nature rocky, with scattered springs and rainfall that is often inadequate, and where the soils mostly are washed down into the wadi bottoms below. When Israel entered these lands, they found the Bronze Age city-states and their dependent villages long in possession of the best sources of water and soil. The Israelite tribes, as we have seen, initially settled the largely empty areas between. Their success in putting down roots in these relatively undeveloped areas was due in part to the use of two productive technologies, terraces and cisterns.[50] Terraces, which are a series of stone walls running horizontally along slope of a hill, trap the natural run-off of soil and water to form long, narrow plots of ground in which orchards of summer fruit thrive. Cisterns are deep, man-made cavities hewn out of bedrock and then plastered and fitted with sealed openings, in which rainwater collects and is stored throughout the year. Both appear in the archaeological record in the hill country during Iron Age I (twelfth and eleventh centuries B.C.), precisely when and where Israel first settled the land. From the Iron Age on, we find many rock-cut installations in the hill country designed to collect, transport and store water, areas of terracing to collect soil, and the remains of olive presses and wine presses to convert raw products to usable forms.[51] There is also archaeological evidence that from the ninth through seventh centuries B.C., Israelite settlement pushed into portions of the arid Negev and Judean Wilderness by means of runoff farming. This technology involved constructing a series of low dams across wadi bottoms, each with long wings running up slope to catch rainfall and direct its waters to small fields in the wadis. By these means, plots of ground that might expect six inches or less of rainwater per year received instead the equivalent of twenty-four inches or more, an amount equal to high hill country sites such as Jerusalem. Runoff farming technology was perfected

Here a cistern and stone hewn trough provide water for flocks and herds in the eastern Benjamin hills. Access to the cistern water is protected by an iron cover.

The terracing in this section of the hill country of Judah near the village of Husan southwest of Bethlehem shows centuries of planning and care, and provides a stable livelihood for its industrious owners.

during the Byzantine Period, when an estimated half-million acres of arid land came under cultivation in the Negev Highlands south of Beer-sheba.

By the time of the Roman Empire the opposite, removing water from plots of ground, was also true. The Romans are famous for transporting water over long distances through aqueducts, and impressive aqueducts are known in the archaeological record that brought water to Jerusalem and to Caesarea from natural springs many miles away. But they also drained swamps by cutting through the *kurkar* ridges of the northern Sharon Plain to reclaim water-logged land that lay to the east. In this way, their new port on the Mediterranean, Caesarea, gained an agricultural hinterland.

Deforestation was a recurring phenomenon throughout the southern Levant in ancient times, with, as might be expected, both productive and harmful results. The alluvial valleys of the Judean Shephelah may have been deforested as early as the Early Bronze Age (c. 3200–2200 B.C.).[52] Joshua 17:14–18 mentions that the tribe of Ephraim cleared the forested hills of their landed inheritance as their population increased, a statement that allows us to see both the natural fertility of the land and its reuse through human inter-vention. The Romans also deforested portions of Judea in order to construct siege works during the Great Revolt of A.D. 66–70; the Garden of Gethsemane, lying just east of Jerusalem, was certainly one of their victims.

The technologies of conveying water to irrigate arid lands and drain swampy ones, to reclaim and enrich the soil, and to open new lands to productive agriculture, were particularly productive during the Iron Age (the time of the Judean and Israelite monarchies), the Byzantine Period, and today. Because in modern times so much of the land has been altered from its natural state, it becomes almost impossible to follow the advice of Sauer and look at the land through the eyes of its former inhabitants. The Sharon Plain, the Jezreel and Harod Valleys, and the Huleh Basin are prime examples of this, areas that today are intensively farmed but in antiquity were given to unproductive, swampy and unhealthy ground.

Cultural ecology examines the tug between technologies that blend in with the environment and those that alter it, and is es-pecially cognizant of processes that are detrimental to land and inhabitant alike. The line drawn between productive and destructive consequences is often blurred, and in the eye of the beholder (or, according to the opinion of the one set to gain the most from their use). The overall progression in the southern Levant has been from unusable land to agrarian-based landscapes, then to urban-based environments that place stress on ecosystems beyond their normal ability to bear. The greater the number of people, the greater the demand for available water and soil resources and the stronger the need to further alter the affected ecosystems in order to keep up. In arid areas such as the Jordan Valley, the Aravah and the Negev Basin today, date palms and fruit trees are becoming dominant while tamarisks and acacias gradually disappear from their native habitat. Citrus groves have supplanted native oak forests on the Sharon Plain, which are in turn being replaced by urban sprawl, asphalt, parking lots and garbage dumps (both legal and illegal).

As human populations increase, the populations of the largest animals, the predators, have decreased. "Man was once surrounded by wild animals," comments Walter Ferguson. "Today, wild animals are surrounded by man."[53] The smaller the animal, and the more nocturnal, the greater its chances for survival. Lions and bears have long ago disappeared from the lands of the Bible;[54] wolves, hyenas and the wild boar remain, but are under pressure from farmers and ranchers who sometimes prefer to protect their livelihood through poisons. The greatest deforestation took place during the Ottoman times, by locals who preferred to cut trees rather than pay a tax on their land based on evidence of its fertility, and to build and fuel the railroads. As the woodlands disappear so do the animals living in them. The Roe Deer, the Mesopotamian Fallow Dear and the Lynx have all disappeared from the northern, Galilee forests. Drain-ing swamps also affects wildlife who once found their home in the swampy areas. Good riddance to the malaria-carrying mosquito, but the Syrian Water Vole also became extinct and the Common Otter is

The waters of the Huleh Nature Reserve preserve a remnant of a much larger lake and swamp that once covered much of the southern Huleh valley north of the Sea of Galilee.

now rare since the draining of the Huleh swamp.

But the movement is not all one direction. Although corroborative archaeological evidence is lacking, it seems as though the ancient Israelites practiced rudimentary methods of soil restoration. The Mosaic law speaks of letting the land lie fallow every seventh year (Ex 23:10–11). This injunction seems to indicate some level of awareness, at least in some parts of ancient Israelite society, that the land needed rest to recover from repeated years of soil depletion.[55] It also served to bind people to land through a shared keeping of the Sabbath. The prohibition of sowing two kinds of seed at the same time in the same soil (Lev 19:19; Deut 22:9) may imply the practice of annual crop rotation.[56] In both cases, however, it is not possible to know to what extent the injunction was actually practiced, or only represented an ideal. Today there is a heightened awareness of all manner of ecological concerns in Israel, and great efforts are made in soil and water conservation, the protection of natural habitats, and the reintroduction and conservation of species that have, over the years, disappeared from the land.

Seeing a land through the eyes of its former inhabitants, as Sauer has advocated, is immensely easier when those inhabitants leave us their texts, and this is the case for the land of ancient Israel. As readers of the Bible we might question just whose views the texts preserve, and wonder whether or not they are representative of ancient Israelite society as a whole. As worthwhile as those conversations might be, the reality is that the principal text that we do have for the inhabitants of the land of ancient Israel is the Bible, and its primary voice is a prophetic one, that is, a voice that seeks to interpret particular moments in time (their own moments, primarily) through a divine perspective.[57] The biblical prophet, in the words of the great twentieth century theologian, philosopher and social critic Abraham J. Heschel, is "a man who feels fiercely.... The prophet is the voice that God has lent to the silent agony, a voice to the plundered poor, to the profaned riches of the world. It is a form of living, a crossing point of God and man."[58] And the biblical prophets, with their incredibly holistic view of life, were unable to separate people from land or Israel's actions from the grounded context on which they took place. Human behavior, the prophets decried, affected not only people and the social structures they created but also the ecosystems in which they lived. The land itself, and all of the natural resources that make human life productive and bountiful, was cursed after Adam's fall and exile from Eden (Gen 3:17–19). That curse was tempered a bit when Joshua entered the land (Deut 11:13–17), but only as far as Israel's actions were consistent with God's guidance as to how they should live. People and land together receive blessing, and judgment. When one suffers, both suffer; when people rejoice, so does their land (Deut 29:22–28; Isa 24:1–23; Hos 4:2–3; Amos 5:14–17). The same God who created the world as a place perfectly suited for human habitation, de-creates it if his people are found to be not worthy to live there (Jer 4:23–29; Amos 1:2; Zeph 1:2–3). As is usually the case, the prophet Isaiah said it best, taking care to mention the specific regions of his land that were, by nature, the most fertile and green:

> Woe to you, O destroyer,
>> while you were not destroyed,
> and he who is treacherous,
>> while others did not deal treacherously with him....
> The land mourns and pines away,
>> Lebanon is shamed and withers;
> Sharon is like a desert plain (Heb. 'aravah),
>> and Bashan and Carmel lose their foliage.

Isaiah 33:1, 9

Then he reversed the image, from curse to blessing, this time starting with the regions of his land that were, by nature, the most arid and brown:

> The wilderness (Heb. midbar) and drought-land (Heb. siyyah)
>> will be glad, and the desert plain (Heb. 'aravah)
>>> will rejoice and blossom like the crocus.
> It will blossom profusely
>> and rejoice with rejoicing and shouts of joy.
> The glory of Lebanon will be given to it,
>> the majesty of Carmel and Sharon.

Isaiah 35:1–2

In binding the physicality of human life to its spiritual dimensions, the prophets were able to speak holistically to the human need to "do justice, love kindness and walk humbly with your God" (Mic 6:8)...in "the land into which you are entering to possess" (Deut 11:10).

F. "A LAND FOR WHICH THE LORD YOUR GOD CARES" —
DEUTERONOMY 11:12

And what of the place name, Promised Land? Although the phrase as such occurs nowhere in the Hebrew Bible, its geographical referent is surely the land of ancient Israel, the place into which God promised to bring his people:

> When you enter the land that the LORD will give you, as He has promised....
>
> Exodus 12:25

The term itself, though, is Christian, transferring the language of the homeland of ancient Israel to a heavenly home in which believers in Christ receive blessings that for all eternity far surpass those they might—or might not—have had on earth.[59] In commenting on God's call that Abraham leave his Haran home and journey to a place unknown to him, the writer of the book of Hebrews perceived that Abraham "was to receive an inheritance...[in] the land of promise," a place where he was looking "for the city which has foundations whose architect and builder is God" (Heb 11:8–10). Amplifying the theme, a veritable Who's Who of Western writers from Augustine to Chaucer to Bunyan to Tennyson and C. S. Lewis crafted narratives of expectation and hope in which a promised land embodied something to be gained in the life to come that far surpassed the things of this world.[60]

The reality is not to be denied, but an equally strong biblical theme is driven by quite a different current: not "a land (and its benefits) that I promise to give you," but rather "a land in which I promise to take care of you, even now." The biblical authors are abundantly clear that this present world and all of its resources belong to God (Lev 25:23; Job 41:11; Ps 24:1; 50:10–11; 89:11). The corollary is that people are stewards of the here and now. One of the implications is that deeds of purchase or rights of use are structures of human convenience to ensure custody over plots of ground for a generation or two. Though cliché, the axiom is true: We are not just inheriting the earth (or our specific purchased plot of it) from our parents, we are borrowing it from our children. The biblical authors were far more concerned about obligations of custodial care than they were about rights of ownership, on both the personal and national level.

> Because they forsook the covenant of the LORD, the God of their fathers [in all of its custodial aspects]...the LORD uprooted them from their land in anger and in fury and in great wrath, and cast them into another land."
>
> Deuteronomy 29:25, 28

And giving custodial care is something that God does best (Ps 65; 104):

> The land into which you are about to cross to possess...is a land for which the LORD your God cares. They eyes of the LORD your God are always on it, from the beginning even to the end of the year.
>
> Deuteronomy 11:11–12

We have seen that this land of promise is both "adequate and bounteous," as described by Elmer Martens, above.[61] Our tendency is to emphasize the term *bounteous* and think of a land without scarcity or lack (Deut 8:9). And, compared to forty years in the wasteland of Sinai, the land of ancient Israel certainly was that. Here, as noted by Walter Bruggemann,[62] water does not come at the last minute from a struck rock but from cycles of rainfall and perennial springs. Here food does not drop mysteriously from the sky or appear after a night's dew but from the tilled ground, according to its season. More difficult to define is the word *adequate*, which has connotations not of plenty, but of enough. And this is the key. We can sense how Israel's homeland, the land of promise, was

adequate by looking at two cycles of time: the **year** and the **week**.

The passage of time over the course of a **year** in the ancient Near East was marked by the natural cycle of seasons and their proper agricultural activities. In Egypt, the year was tied to the rise and fall of the floodwaters of the Nile which brought renewed topsoil and water for irrigation to the river's narrow basin. Ancient Egypt's three seasons were *akhet*, "inundation," *peret*, "emergence," and *shemu*, "dryness." The yearly calendar in Mesopotamia was tied to the annual rainy season / dry season sequence and the agricultural activities that took place in each. The Canaanites, indigenous inhabitants of the Levant, ordered their calendar like those of Mesopotamia, since their land, too, experienced an annual cycle of wet and dry months. A tenth century B.C. text found at Gezer reckons their year as beginning with the ingathering of the late summer fruit (olives) in late fall. This coincides with the expectation of the early (autumn) rains.

> His two months: ingathering [Sept–Oct—Oct–Nov]
> His two months: sowing [Nov–Dec—Dec–Jan]
> His two months: late sowing [Jan–Feb—Feb–Mar]
> His month: flax cutting [Mar–Apr]
> His month: barley harvest [Apr–May]

Irrigation has been the method of watering fields in Egypt for millennia, bringing the water of the Nile to desert tracts along its banks and renewing the soil in the process.

45

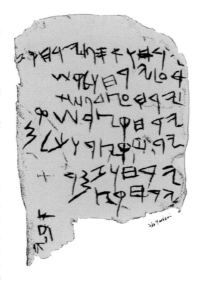

The Gezer Calendar (facsimile), tenth century B.C. (drawing Ada Yardeni).

His month: [wheat] harvest and measuring [May–June]
His two months: vine harvest [June–July—July–Aug]
His month: summer [fruit] harvest [Aug–Sept].[63]

Israel's calendar followed the same general pattern, though according to the narrative of the first Passover their year would begin in the spring (Ex 12:1–2), with what corresponded to the beginning of the barley harvest up in Canaan. The Hebrew name of their first month was *Aviv* (*Abib*), a term that designates the first ripe grain of barley (Ex 9:31; 13:4; 23:15; 34:18; Deut 16:1).[64] It was during their years in exile that Israel adopted the Babylonian month names, which are preserved as the names of the months of the Jewish calendar today. In doing so, *Aviv* became *Nisan*, from the name of the corresponding Babylonian month *Nisannu*, "the first produce of the season." Israel's three great pilgrimage festivals, which celebrated their great national founding epic, were tied to the agricultural festivals that occurred at natural turning points within the agricultural cycle of Canaan: the Exodus from Egypt (*Pesach* or Passover) at the time of the Feast of Unleavened Bread which coincided with the beginning of the barley harvest; the giving of Torah on Mount Sinai (*Shavuot* or Weeks) at the Feast of Harvest marking the end of the wheat harvest; and God's provision during the forty years of Wilderness Wanderings (*Succot* or Booths) at the Feast of Ingathering of the summer fruit (Ex 23:14–17; Deut 16:1–17).

This historical-geographical reality helped to fuse Israel the people to Israel the land, with all sorts of crucial ramifications. The primary implication for our attempt to understand the *adequacy* of that land is that, in the Bible, God's care for land becomes a metaphor for the way that he cares for the people who live on the land. People, the writer of Deuteronomy declares, have an inheritance, a place to call home:

> When the Most High gave the nations their inheritance,
>   when he separated the sons of man,
> He set the boundaries of the peoples
>   according to the number of the sons of Israel.

> Deuteronomy 32:8

But what is God's inheritance? People.

> But the LORD's portion is His people;
>   Jacob is the allotment of His inheritance.

> Deuteronomy 32:9

If we choose to emphasize the *bounteous* aspect of the land of promise and understand the term promise to embrace things gotten or benefits gained, there is a significant disconnect between the Bible's statements that God cares for people and land and the ecological facts on the ground that Israel called home.

It all comes back to rainfall. While the weather patterns of the southern Levant are generally repetitive, exactly when the early rains might begin, and how much rain might actually fall during the winter months any given year, is always unpredictable (Amos 4:7–9). The ancient Israelite farmer's expectation that he would harvest a crop large enough to pay taxes to his (usually) rapacious government, be able to purchase necessities at a fair price in the market (Amos 4:1; 8:4–6), and still have enough left over to feed his family for the year was never guaranteed and often unfulfilled. The Bible speaks of times of famine that caused people to seek food in other lands (Gen 12:10; 26:1; 41:57; Ruth 1:1), but these are only the most severe instances of what was an annual peril. The end of every harvest cycle held the potential of famine, with two "hungry gaps"[65] a year, the month prior the barley harvest and the month just before the harvest of summer fruit. It was at these points in time that the stores of food from the prior year were at their lowest point, and likely dried out, infested, molded or rotten.

"What makes bitter things sweet?" asked Alciun, the Yorkshire schoolmaster who went to reform Frankish education for the emperor Charlemagne in the eighth century. "Hunger."[66]

The writers of the Bible, those who allow us to see the land of ancient Israel through the eyes of its former inhabitants, knew all of this of course, and that their promised land wasn't, in the end, the easiest place to live.

But wasn't theirs "a land flowing with milk and honey?" This refrain punctuates the Pentateuch with anticipation (Ex 3:8, 17; 13:5; 33:3; Lev 20:24; Num 13:27; 14:8; 16:13–14; Deut 6:3; 11:9; 26:9, 15; 27:3; 31:20; Josh 5:6; cf. Jer 11:5; 32:22; Ezek 20:6, 15). A tremendous amount of hermeneutical attention has been given to understanding this phrase as indicating a land overflowing with goodness and plenty (a modern equivalent might be "health and wealth" or "stocks and bonds"). Yet we must not overlook the fact that "milk" and "honey" are the best products of the shepherd and the farmer, respectively, and that these two people groups learned to a forge living from two very different ecosystems.[67] Both adapted well to their chosen environments, though the shepherd's life is lived on a much thinner, and hence more vulnerable, base of resources. Perhaps the phrase "land of milk and honey" is meant to recall that the land of promise embodies two very different living situations, one (the land of the farmer where "honey" abounds) relatively well blessed by material resources and the other (the land of the shepherd where "milk" is the primary means of protein) much less so. Both need the other to survive; both are subject, in their own way, to the threats that lay beyond their control; and both, by themselves, are adequate—not with plenty, but with enough.

We can also understand something about the adequacy of the land of ancient Israel by considering the cycle of time that we call the **week**. Of all of the recurring cycles of time, it is the week that doesn't fit observable natural phenomena. The Hebrew day is measured by the setting of the sun, the month by the appearance of the new moon, and the year by counting twelve new moons and watching for the first ripe barley. (In the Hebrew calendar a thirteenth month is added every two or three years in order to bring the lunar calendar back into sync with movement of the sun, which determines the growing seasons.) The seven-day week, though, does not correspond to any exact observable natural phenomena. While its origins are debated,[68] a plain reading of the biblical text couches the seven-day week within the context of creation (Ex 20:8–11), with the week standing apart from mere natural phenomena and hence making it more significant than other ways of reckoning the passage of time.[69] And, because the week is imbedded in creation, it becomes the cycle that most effectively binds time to place, with the seventh day, the Sabbath (*Shabbat*), a day that embraces God, his creative activity and the eternal present.[70] The weekly celebration of the Sabbath is a continual reminder that the living conditions of Eden are not something of the hoary past, but attainable, or if not attainable, at least approachable, and that in the meantime the world is sustained by the ongoing care of God.

It is here that we should pause to consider the significance of three of the greatest milestones in the development of religious thought.

The first is monotheism; the second is that the One God who exists is a being who is ontologically (or, of essence) different from the physical world which he made. These two tenets stand in stark contrast to the religious thought of the world in which ancient Israel lived. In the ancient Near East, the divine realms were conceived as being inhabited by multiple deities, all of whom were coextensive or continuous to some degree with the physical worlds which they had made.[71] This made them party to the foibles of humankind. The third milestone is that unlike the deities of the ancient Near East who tended to exploit the physical world for their own good, the defining attitude and primary activity of the One God of the Bible is to care for his creation, especially people. The earth is our mother in the sense that we draw strength and sustenance from the resources that it provides. It is not our Mother, itself divine, from whom life flows. That attribute is reserved for God alone.

The Genesis creation account describes a specially prepared land called the Garden of (or, in) Eden (Gen 2:8, 15), in which people (initially, and ultimately, only two) could talk and walk (Gen 3:8) with God. Much of the language that describes the garden was picked up by later biblical writers to describe the land of Israel, Jerusalem and/or the tabernacle and the temple.[72] Some of the statements are obvious:

> Indeed, the LORD will comfort Zion;
>   He will comfort all her waste places.
> And her wilderness (Heb. midbar) He will make like Eden,
>   and her desert like the garden of the LORD.
>
> Isaiah 51:3
>
> They will say, "This desolate land [the land of Israel] has become like the garden of Eden."
>
> Ezekiel 36:35
>
> The land is like the Garden of Eden before them.
>
> Joel 2:3

Others are more subtle. The gold and precious stones of Eden (Gen 2:12) are also found in the tabernacle and temple furnishings (Ex 28:6–30; 1 Chron 29:2; Hag 2:7–8; Rev 21:18, 20); the name Gihon, the name of one of the four rivers of Eden, (Gen 2:13) is otherwise known only as the spring of Jerusalem (1 Kgs 1:38); the "cool (Heb. ruah, "wind") of the day" (Gen 3:8) is especially noticeable in the higher elevations of the hill country; figs (Gen 3:7) and thorns and thistles (Gen 3:18) are familiar plants in the hills of Israel's home, a place that is otherwise called "a good land" (Deut 8:7), with "good" the repeated refrain defining each day of creation (Gen 1:10, 12, 18, 25, 31). We can put it this way: those who try to put the Garden of Eden on a modern map nearly always place it somewhere in southern Mesopotamia, at the confluence of the Tigris and Euphrates rivers, no doubt influenced by parallels in the Genesis creation account with the Babylonian creation epic, *Enuma Elish*.[73] Much better to follow the internal language of the Bible and to recognize that the place where God and people first lived together in ecological wholeness was the place on the globe that would later become the land of Israel.

We could argue that the biblical writers chose to describe Eden with language that they already knew from Jerusalem, rather than the other way around, in order to create a proper primeval setting for their city, but the result is the same: Eden and Jerusalem share a common essence. One place is intended to be reminiscent of the other. Is the ecology of Jerusalem and the hill country of Judah harsh and unpredictable? Yes, but if so, it is nevertheless adequate because it represents a return to Eden. Whatever the original inhabitants of Eden had in terms of things, it was enough; so too in Jerusalem. Both were places where God was. The template of life the way it was supposed to be for the average Israelite, with everyone under their own vine and fig tree (1 Kgs 4:25), was also an ecology of

Sunrise from Mount Sinai (Jebel Musa).

> …I brought their weakness to the mountain's goal,
> Into the bare immensities of God.
>
> *Moses Speaks*, by Amy Blank, 1959.

sufficiency—not of plenty, but of enough. So the proverb, which recognizes that in its natural state the land of Israel is neither abject nothingness (a desert wasteland) nor a funnel for riches (as was Phoenicia). Rather, in its geopolitical position, its climate, its available resources and in its cultural ecology, it is something in between:

> Give me neither poverty nor riches;
>   feed me with the food that is my portion,
> that I not be full and deny You and say, "Who is the LORD?"
>   or that I not be in want and steal.
>
> Proverbs 30:8–9

When we read Scripture we learn to read Creation. It is possible to secularize both by adopting a materialistic approach to nature and a humanistic approach to Scripture, where natural forces of survival give shape to the land and the agendacized choices of editors give shape to the text. But the Bible itself insists otherwise. Chief among its voices is the insistence that because God cares for the land and people that he made, people should care for their land and each other as well.

Howard Snyder, a Christian theologian with a strong sense of environmental responsibility, has identified four false readings of the natural world.[74] The first is romanticizing nature, that is, believing that the most essential elements of truth are found in the beauty of nature. The second is commodifying nature, holding that real value in the natural world is found in its products or its use as property. The third is worshipping nature, finding in it the highest values of life; and the fourth is spiritualizing nature by overriding its physical value to point to external spiritual truths only. More helpful is to read nature (of which people are a part) in dialogue with Scripture. Both point to God; both provide templates to help people better understand and embrace the other.

Too often, Bible readers who say "This world is not my home; I'm just a passin' through"[75] have tended to deemphasize serious environmentalism, while those holding the opposite position, "this world is all we've got so we'd better take care of it" have leaned toward self-actualized mother earth spiritualities. A Genesis to Revelation sweep of biblical voices recognizes a reality that is greater than the sum of these parts.

47

NOTES AND REFERENCES

1 The reference is not to the writers of individual sources, or pieces, of the biblical text, but to the unknown persons or groups of persons responsible for the compositional form of the Hebrew Bible and, subsequently, the New Testament.

2 Jeff Malpas, *Place and Experience: A Philosophical Topography* (Cambridge: Cambridge University Press, 1999), 15–16; and Cynthia Parker, "Deuteronomy's Place: An Analysis of the Placial Structure of Deuteronomy," unpublished Ph.D. dissertation, University of Gloucestershire, 2014, 1.

3 The English word ecology is derived from Greek *oikos*, "house" or "dwelling place" and hence "environment."

4 Elmer Martens, *God's Design: A Focus on Old Testament Theology* (Grand Rapids, Mich.: Baker Book House, 1981, 29).

5 Walter Brueggemann, *The Land* (Philadelphia: Fortress Press, 1977), 47–53.

6 Brueggemann, 53–59.

7 Bargil Pixner, *With Jesus through Galilee according to the Fifth Gospel* (Rosh Pina: Corazin Publishing, 1992).

8 Yohanan Aharoni, *The Land of the Bible: A Historical Geography* (Philadelphia: Westminster Press, 1979), 108–10; Oded Borowski, *Agriculture in Iron Age Israel* (Boston: American Schools of Oriental Research, 2002), 12–14.

9 James B. Pritchard, ed., *Ancient Near Eastern Texts Relating to the Old Testament* (Princeton: Princeton University Press, 1955), 19.

10 Strabo, *The Geography of Strabo*. Transl. by Horace Leonard Jones. Loeb Classical Library (Cambridge: Harvard University Press, 1917), xvi.2.36.

11 See for instance Eveline van der Steen, *Near Eastern Tribal Societies during the Nineteenth Century: Economy, Society and Politics between Tent and Town* (Sheffield: Equinox, 2013); Charles E. Carter, "Opening Windows into Biblical Worlds: Applying Social Sciences to Hebrew Scripture." Pg. 421–451 in David W. Baker and Bill T. Arnold, eds., *The Face of Old Testament Studies: A Survey of Contemporary Approaches* (Grand Rapids, Mich.: Baker, 1999), and Karen Seger, ed., *Portrait of a Palestinian Village: The Photographs of Hilma Grandqvist* (London: The Third World Centre for Research and Publishing, 1981).

12 Suggestions include the meadow saffron, crocus, narcissus, white lily, anemone, tulip and, based on Akkadian *habatsillatu*, a "fresh shoot of reed."

13 Borowski, *Agriculture*, 12–14; Yohanan Aharoni, *The Land of the Bible* (Philadelphia: Westminster Press, 1979), 109–110.

14 See for example Michael Zohary, *Plants of the Bible* (Cambridge: Cambridge University Press, 1982); Oded Borowski, *Every Living Thing: Daily Use of Animals in Ancient Israel* (Walnut Creek, Cal.: Altamira Press, 1998); Harold N. Moldenke and Alma L. Moldenke, *Plants of the Bible* (New York: Dover Publications, 1952); George Cansdale, *Animals of Bible Lands* (Devon: Paternoster Press, 1970); *Fauna and Flora of the Bible: Helps for Translators*, 2d. ed. (London: United Bible Societies, 1980); Nogah Hareuveni, *Tree and Shrub in Our Biblical Heritage*, transl. by Helen Frenkley (Kiryat Ono: Neot Kedumim, 1984); and Nohag Hareuveni, *Desert and Shepherd in Our Biblical Heritage* (Lod: Neot Kedumim, 1991); Borowski, *Agriculture*, 87–139; Ami Tamir, *Sacred Flowers, Holy Trees & Blessed Thorns* (Jerusalem: Carta, 2017).

15 Pliny, *Natural History*. Transl. by H. Rackham. Loeb Classical Library (Cambridge: Harvard University Press, 1969), 5.xv.71.

16 Pliny, *Natural History*. 5.xv.70.

17 Strabo, *Geography*, xvii.1.51.

18 Strabo, *Geography*, xvi.2.29.

19 Strabo, *Geography*, xvi.2.27–28.

20 Josephus, *The Jewish War*. Transl. by H. St. J. Thackeray. Loeb Classical Library (Cambridge: Harvard University Press, 1961), iii.506–521.

21 Pritchard, *ANET*, 477–478.

22 James Henry Breasted, *Ancient Records of Egypt: Historical Documents*, Vol. II: *The Eighteenth Dynasty* (Chicago: University of Chicago Press, 1906), 196.

23 Breasted, *Ancient Records of Egypt*, 187–217.

24 The most complete collection is found in Shmuel Aḥituv, *Echoes from the Past: Hebrew and Cognate Inscriptions from the Biblical Period* (Jerusalem: Carta, 2008). Also helpful is Wayne Horowitz, Takayoshi Oshima and Seth Sanders, *Cuneiform in Canaan: Cuneiform Sources from the Land of Israel in Ancient Times* (Jerusalem: Israel Exploration Society, 2006).

25 Aḥituv, *Echoes from the Past*, 438–439.

26 Zohary, *Plants of the Bible*, 14.

27 H. B. Tristram, *The Survey of Western Palestine: The Flora and Fauna of Palestine* (London: Committee of the Palestine Exploration Fund, 1885).

28 Gustaf Dalman, *Arbeit und Sitte in Palästina*, 8 vols. (Gütersloh: C. Bertelsmann, 1928); Vol. 1/1 and 1/2 translated as *Work and Customs in Palestine* by Nadia Abdulhadi-Sukhtian (Ramallah: Dar al Nasher, 2013).

29 Lidar Sapir-Hen, "Pigs as an Ethnic Marker? You Are What You Eat." *Biblical Archaeology Review* 42/6 (2016): 41–43, 70.

30 Ronny Reich, Eli Shukron and Omri Lernau, "Recent Discoveries in the City of David, Jerusalem," *Israel Exploration Journal*, 57/2 (2007): 153–169.

31 Borowski, *Agriculture*, 47–139.

32 R. A. Schwaller de Lubicz, *The Temples of Karnak* (London: Thames & Hudson, 1999), 633–639.

33 Yigal Shiloh, *The Proto-Aeolic Capital and Israelite Ashlar Masonry*. QEDEM 11 (Jerusalem: Hebrew University Institute of Archaeology, 1979), 26–49.

34 Amihai Mazar, *Archaeology of the Land of the Bible: 10,000–586 B.C.E.* (New York: Doubleday, 1990), 455–458.

35 Zohary, *Plants of the Bible*, 13.

36 Oded Borowski, *Daily Life in Biblical Times* (Leiden: Brill, 2003), 63–74.

37 John A. Beck, gen. ed., *Zondervan Dictionary of Biblical Imagery* (Grand Rapids: Mich.: Zondervan, 2011), 85.

38 Mark Twain, *The Innocent's Abroad* (New York: New American Library Signet Classic, 1966), 401.

39 Amihai Mazar, Dvory Namdar, Nava Panitz-Cohen, Ronny Neumann and Steve Weiner, "The Iron Age II Beehives at Tel Rehov in the Jordan Valley: Archaeological and Analytical Aspects," *Antiquity* 82 (2008): 629–639. DNA analysis of the beehives found at Tel Rehov indicates that their bees were imported from Anatolia (Turkey) and that they produced a superior kind of honey.

40 Mazar, *Archaeology*, 269–270.

41 K. A. Kitchen, *On the Reliability of the Old Testament* (Grand Rapids, Mich.: Eerdmans, 2003), 338–339.

42 For a comparative view, see Jean Bottéro, *The Oldest Cuisine in the World: Cooking in Mesopotamia*. Transl. by Teresa Lavender Fagan (Chicago: University of Chicago Press, 2004).

43 For a quick summary of some suggestions see W. J. Houston, "Foods, Clean and Unclean," pg. 326–336 in *Dictionary of the Old Testament: Pentateuch*, eds. T. Desmond Alexander and David W. Baker (Downer's Grove, Ill.: InterVarsity Press, 2003). Note also Avraham Faust, *Israel's Ethnogenesis: Settlement, Interaction, Expansion and Resistance* (London: Equinox, 2006), 35–40.

44 Carl Ortwin Sauer, "Forward to Historical Geography," in *Land and Life: A Selection from the Writings of Carl Ortwin Sauer*, ed. John Leighly (Berkeley: University of California Press, 1963), 360.

45 Sauer, "Forward to Historical Geography," 362.

46 M. B. Rowton, "Dimorphic Structure and Topology." *Oriens Antiquus* 15 (1976): 17–31.

47 Anson F. Rainey and R. Steven Notley, *The Sacred Bridge: Carta's Atlas of the Biblical World*. 2d. emended & enhanced ed. (Jerusalem: Carta, 2014), 179.

48 Anson Rainey, personal communication.

49 Borowski, *Every Living Thing*, 61–62.

50 Borowski, *Agriculture*, 15.

51 Shimon Gibson and Gershon Edelstein, "Investigating Jerusalem's Rural Landscape." *Levant* XVII (1985): 139–155.

52 John D. Currid, "The Deforestation of the Foothills of Palestine." *Palestine Exploration Quarterly* 166 (1984): 1–11.

53 Walter W. Ferguson, *The Mammals of Israel* (Jerusalem: Gefen, 2002), 17.

54 Cansdale, *Animals of Bible Lands*, 106–107, 116–117. Lions apparently disappeared from Palestine during the time of the Crusades although some Western travels report spottings as late as the nineteenth century. The last Syrian Bear in Palestine, once common in the higher elevations, was killed just prior to the Second World War. Others remain in the mountainous regions of Lebanon and Syria.

55 Borowski, *Agriculture*, 143–145.

56 Borowski, *Agriculture*, 148–149.

57 Abraham Joshua Heschel, *The Prophets: An Introduction*. Vol. 1. (New York: Harper & Row, 1962), xiii–xiv.

58 Heschel, *The Prophets*, 5.

59 Robert L. Wilken, *The Land Called Holy: Palestine in Christian History & Thought* (New Haven: Yale University Press, 1992), 127–128; David Lyle Jeffrey, gen. ed. *A Dictionary of Biblical Tradition in English Literature* (Grand Rapids: Eerdmans, 1992), 255.

60 See Jeffrey, *Dictionary of Biblical Tradition*, 254–260, for a summary.

61 Endnote 4.

62 Brueggemann, *The Land*, 49.

63 Aḥituv, *Echoes from the Past*, 254.

64 Alex Strashny, "Modern Searches for Aviv Barley in the Context of the Hebrew Calendar: A First Description of the Israeli Barley Observation Data," *The Jewish Bible Quarterly* 45:3 (2017): 179–187.

65 Del Sweeney, ed., *Agriculture in the Middle Ages* (Philadelphia: University of Pennsylvania Press, 1995), 227.

66 Robert Lacey and Danny Danziger, *The Year 1000: What Life was Like at the Turn of the First Millennium* (London: Little, Brown and Company, 1999), 57.

67 John A. Beck, *The Land of Milk and Honey* (St. Louis, Concordie, 2006), 11.

68 Roland deVaux, *Ancient Israel*, vol. 2: *Religious Institutions* (New York: McGraw-Hill, 1965), 475–483.

69 Abraham Joshua Heschel, *The Sabbath*. (Boston: Shambhala, 2003), xviii.

70 Heschel, *The Sabbath*, 59–65.

71 John N. Oswalt, *The Bible Among the Myths* (Grand Rapids, Mich.: Zondervan, 2009), 47–84.

72 Gordon J. Wenham, "Sanctuary Symbolism in the Garden of Eden Story," *Proceedings of the World Congress of Jewish Studies* 9 (1986): 16–25.

73 Alexander Heidel, *The Babylonian Genesis*, 2d. ed. (Chicago: University of Chicago Press, 1951).

74 Howard A. Snyder, *Salvation Means Creation Healed* (Eugene, Ore.: Cascade Books, 2011), 42–45; cited in Daniel L. Brunner, Jennifer J. Butler and A. J. Swoboda, *Introducing Evangelical Ecotheology: Foundations in Scripture, Theology, History, and Praxis* (Grand Rapids, Mich.: Baker Academic, 2014), 24.

75 The title of a hymn by Albert E. Brumley, 1937.